The Influential Legends of Soul Music: The Lives of Sam Cooke, Otis Redding, Marvin Gaye, Aretha Franklin, and Stevie Wonder

By Charles River Editors

Sam Cooke

About Charles River Editors

Charles River Editors provides superior editing and original writing services across the digital publishing industry, with the expertise to create digital content for publishers across a vast range of subject matter. In addition to providing original digital content for third party publishers, we also republish civilization's greatest literary works, bringing them to new generations of readers via ebooks.

Sign up here to receive updates about free books as we publish them, and visit Our Kindle Author Page to browse today's free promotions and our most recently published Kindle titles.

John McCormack. If he had been born Italian, he might have starred in the refined, lyrical Mozart opera roles usually reserved for those with an extreme musical sensitivity. Such was the level of excellence in Cooke's inner understanding of his own voice, which was capable of exquisite classical precision and a finesse in phrasing that lay far beyond the norm. He could have prospered and attained greatness in any genre of his choice, but considering the timing of the American audience, and his African-American heritage, Sam Cooke instead pioneered a new genre and became its greatest practitioner by blending black musical traditions that incorporated all the refinement and beauty of European classical genres yet still spoke from the heart of his rural American roots.

Record producer John Wexler was more than accurate when he summed up Sam Cooke's talent as a complete package: "It was all there – the exquisite exact intonation, the sovereign control of tone and timbre, the command of the subtlest pitch shadings, bends and slurs." Wexler is in general agreement with the rest of the professional music world and the listening public, whether the term is absolutely understood or not, that Cooke, among all his contemporaries, was "unequalled for sheer musicality."

The timing of Cooke's appearance was perfect, coming as it did at a historical intersection where blues, jazz, country, gospel, and numerous traditional black forms met on the verge of transforming into new musical blends that included rock and new variant forms of jazz. In this genre, soul music, Cooke, above all others, had what it took to lead its ascent in the American pop music industry. As a masterful singer of any of the stylistic blends that went into soul, bringing the older forms along with him, and as both a songwriter and entrepreneur, Cooke would prove to be "one of the most influential black vocalists of the post-World War II period."[1] But unlike some artists who excel in and father new genres, only to achieve fame later as the audience catches up, Cooke immediately cemented his own success and legacy in addition to that of the musical form itself. As a live performer, a "trailblazing recording artist,"[2] and armed with a fine sense of business, he was, through his savvy and persistence, "the first African-American to reach number one on both charts, pop and Rhythm & Blues – [a] fiercely independent musician."[3]

Sam Cooke's legacy can be found both within the musical and in the inner workings and procedures of his industry, after dozens of high-profile African American artists followed his lead, and obtained new freedom and profit from their own work. As a singer who sold ten million copies as a crossover artist, he set a high vocal bar for all those who came after, and his artistic personality and "suave, sophisticated image set the style of soul crooners for the next decade."[4] "A number of artists in the following generation who were either directly launched by

[1] David Ritz, Encyclopaedia Britannica, Sam Cooke – www.britannica.com/EBchecked/topic/136091/Sam-Cooke/93148/works

[2] Bio.com, Sam Cooke Biography – Singer, Songwriter (1931 – 1954) – www.biography.com/people/sam-cooke-9256129#synopsis

[3] Peter Guralnick, "Dream Boogie: The Triumph of Sam Cooke, Review by Morris S. Levy", in *Notes*, Music Library Association, Vol. 63 No. 1, September, 2006, p. 98

[4] History of Rock, Sam Cooke

Introduction

Sam Cooke (1931-1964)

"I think the secret is really observation. Well, if you observe what's going on and try to figure out how people are thinking, I think you can always write something that people will understand." – Sam Cooke

If Sam Cooke, one of the greatest African-American soul singers in the genre's history, had been Irish, he might have kept company with the likes of the great balladeer and classical tenor his musical influence, mentorship, or producing skills, included many of the newly-emerging stars, such as Smokey Robinson, James Taylor, Michael Jackson, Aretha Franklin, his protégé Bobby Womack, Curtis Mayfield, Stevie Wonder, Marvin Gaye, Otis Redding, and James Brown."[5]

Otis Redding (1941-1967)

"If you want to be a singer, you've got to concentrate on it twenty-four hours a day. You can't be a well driller, too. You've got to concentrate on the business of entertaining and writing songs. Always think different from the next person. Don't ever do a song as you heard somebody else do it." – Otis Redding

At a time when the studios of Motown were turning out one sophisticated, well-groomed artist after another, reinforced by the latest studio technology and benefitting from a powerful marketing system, a parallel industry of more traditionally grounded soul music was also thriving, much of it in the city of Memphis, as represented by artists such as Otis Redding and Stax Records, the label with which Redding would eventually create six studio albums, 30

---

[5] Starpulse.com, Sam Cooke Biography – www.starpulse.com/music/Cooke_Sam/Biography

singles, worldwide fame and a stellar musical legacy.

To some, the Stax Records model may have lagged behind Motown in terms of modernity, with its adherence to older musical and technological modes, but in actuality, Otis Redding and his musical circle represented a preservation movement of sorts, and "exemplified to many listeners the power of Southern 'deep soul' – hoarse, gritty vocals, brassy arrangements, and an emotional way with both party tunes and aching ballads."[6] Such was the perfect conduit for an artist like Otis Redding, who felt compelled by the lifelong urge to sing, years before his dreams of a professional life would ever be realized. And, as the edifice of soul broke further into sub-styles, Redding seemed able to succeed in every one of them.

Once reaching the stage, and becoming increasingly known to the genre's growing public, Redding appeared throughout the United States, Canada, Europe, and the Caribbean, standing "among the biggest box office smashes of any touring performer during his time."[7] As a live performer and recording artist, Redding developed into a master producer, arranger and talent scout as well for pop, soul and R&B and, in time, came to exert a greater control over his own destiny by heading up his own recording studio, Jotis Records, and his own publishing company, Redwal Music. The publishing wing, over a brief period, gained the rights to over 200 commercially distributed songs, some of which would later sell copies numbering in the millions.

Unlike other public figures in the arts, Otis Redding had a logical and clear mind for business, and in only a few years, he was able to parlay his meager beginnings into a recording and publishing company, not to mention the Big "O" Ranch in Georgia, where he would spend some of his most cherished family time. Although the "proudly confessed country boy [with the] big gravelly voice"[8] never reached above #21 on the pop charts' top 40 until the end of his life and career, his appearances "incited pandemonium through the thunderous intensity of his performances, which included vocal ad-libs and false endings,"[9] a free-wheeling improvisatory approach to everything in the moment. It is thought by some that the general public was not quite prepared for Otis Redding the unscripted free spirit, nor was it thoroughly familiar with the purity of soul's rural, Southern roots, not yet a major industry for the country or the world. His stage style, perhaps, was "too intensely soulful for the mainstream market of that time,"[10] and, some have thought, that his true breakthrough into greatness was accomplished only days before his death with the iconic and less soul-oriented "(Sittin' On) The Dock of the Bay." In this departure from the traditional style of his Macon childhood, Redding's most famous piece is not about one-to-one love, but about life itself, and it would go on to break the pop chart curse, "stay[ing] high in the rankings for four weeks."[11]

---

[6] MSN Entertainment, Otis Redding Biography: Soul Ambassador – www.msn.com/music/artist-biographyt/otis-redding/
[7] Otis Redding, the King of Soul – www.otisredding.com/#&panel1-9
[8] Rock & Roll Hall of Fame, Otis Redding Biography
[9] Rock & Roll Hall of Fame, Otis Redding Biography
[10] Rock & Roll Hall of Fame, Otis Redding Biography

The tragic timing of his death robbed Redding of the chance to parlay his success to the next level, but in retrospect, later audiences have not experienced him as either behind the times or inordinately modern. In "I've Been Loving You Too Long," Redding defines and redefines the term "soul man," and he is widely regarded by the 21st century as a "singer of such commanding stature that…he embodies the essence of soul music in its purest form."[12] What was so original and untested in the beginning for the wider audience now occupied a place within its mainstream interests as the new soul forms became more clearly understood. Through his most popular effort, "(Sittin' On) The Dock of the Bay," and by a later review of his entire body of work, Redding is also regarded as one of the premier songwriters and arrangers of his era. In both areas, he had "an enormous talent, [not to mention] a hard-working nature and generous disposition."[13]

Marvin Gaye (1939-1984)

"Great artists suffer for the people." – Marvin Gaye

---

[11] Rock & Roll Hall of Fame, Otis Redding Biography
[12] Rock & Roll Hall of Fame, Otis Redding Biography
[13] Rock & Roll Hall of Fame, Otis Redding Biography

Among the many stars gathered by Berry Gordy's Motown Records during the latter half of the 20th century, one of the most famous and successful was Marvin Gaye, even though the rigidity of the studio's operating procedures constantly collided with his capacity for stubbornness and insistence that he be given the independence to pursue his own artistic vision. Of course, it's easy to see it from both sides; despite the ceaseless thread of masterpieces emerging from Motown studio artists (many of them performed and recorded by Gaye), it might also be said in his defense that as part of the record company's mission statement, Motown operated in a state of near artistic lockdown where creative input by the artist was concerned. Unapologetically hit-driven, Motown measured success almost solely by chart rankings and units sold, and it naturally avoided any alteration of old formulas that produced results, all of which made Motown the epitome of an efficiently-run music entertainment provider. As Marvin Gaye learned, however, it was not the place in which to nourish his thirst for creative freedom and innovation. To further serve the Motown founder's vision, even the associated "charm school" of Maxine Powell was designed to train the singers to carry themselves well in any public situation, in accordance with the Motown mission. Gaye considered such a confining regimen to be worse than useless, and he showed no hesitation in saying so. He once complained, "I am not going to be dictated to by fans, certainly. I am dictated enough to by my record company to last me a million years."

In the construct of Berry Gordy's vision, only the most successful Motown artists could protest or plead for creative expansion, and concessions were far from guaranteed. Motown made the careers of many famous artists, and they subsequently became household names across America, but it very often served as a studio from which many would move on and branch out once their credentials were established. In dealing with the rare artist and personality of Marvin Gaye, however, Motown met the one individual who could resist and even reshape the studio's model without leaving, at least until very late in his career.

That said, while *What's Going On* bucked the trend so far as Motown was concerned, it can also be said that Gaye himself shaped Motown's signature sound with hits like "How Sweet It Is (To Be Loved By You)" and "I Heard It Through the Grapevine." Of course, Gaye also influenced the music industry as a whole, particularly the R&B genre. *Midnight Love* and the hit song "Sexual Healing" are classics that remain instantly recognizable today, and the sound can certainly be heard in the works of subsequent artists.

Gaye's recording career was full of turbulence, and so was his personal life, a point tragically driven home by the fact that he was shot and killed by his own father the day before his 45th birthday. Before his untimely death, Gaye battled all kinds of demons, including drug abuse and depression, and he had stormy relationships with many of the most important figures in his life. If anything, the chaos surrounding him makes his incredible musical career all the more amazing.

Aretha Franklin (1942-)

"Being the Queen is not all about singing, and being a diva is not all about singing. It has much to do with your service to people. And your social contributions to your community and your civic contributions as well." – Aretha Franklin

A certain inevitability characterizes the rise to fame of Aretha Franklin. Indeed, while it is true that neither of her parents were pop singers, they were each talented vocalists—Aretha's father, C.L., was a particularly famous preacher, with a voice so melodic that his sermons effectively doubled as musical performances. Moreover, in an age in which economic opportunities were particularly limited for African-Americans, Aretha was fortunate enough to grow up in a household of relative comfort. Not only was she exposed to music on a daily basis in her household, but her father was a savvy enough businessman to orchestrate her career during its nascent stages, helping her navigate the challenges of entering the music industry. To be certain, in many respects, Aretha Franklin was from an early age the beneficiary of opportunities that are simply unavailable to most aspiring vocalists.

At the same time, it is also clear that in quite obvious ways, Aretha Franklin diverted from her parents and, indeed, important aspects of her racial and cultural heritage. Where her father's musical performances were directly related to his faith, Aretha was a pop singer rather than a gospel one. Her musical style was heavily influenced by the musical traditions of gospel, but she also incorporated aspects of rock and other more popular idioms, an important decision that granted her a far wider audience than she could otherwise have hoped to acquire. As much as Franklin's family upbringing prepared her for a career as a vocalist, her decision to break away from the musical tradition that defined her youth also positions her as something of a maverick. Further, while she certainly enjoyed a far greater audience than her father, this also carried its own challenges in a tumultuous era that saw first the Civil Rights Movement and then Second Wave Feminism. More than just someone who was prepared for success from an early age, Aretha Franklin became very much her own person, a socially- and politically-committed individual invested in promoting social change.

Stevie Wonder (1950-)

Stevie Wonder in 1973

"Just because a man lacks the use of his eyes doesn't mean he lacks vision." – Stevie Wonder

Among the most innovative and independent artists to come out of Motown in the latter half of the 20th century, along with colleagues Marvin Gaye, Isaac Hayes, and Michael Jackson, Stevie Wonder was said by many to possess three distinct obstacles to fulfillment in the music industry. First, he was poor, and worse, he was black and blind. Wonder, however, refused to shrink from or acknowledge any of these realities as barriers, asserting that he had not been in any way disadvantaged or limited in his path toward success.

Through a long and prodigious career at Motown, and a vast experience of collaborations with great musicians of the era, Stevie Wonder has gone on to prove that his optimistic view toward life and work was correct from the very beginning, in a lengthy and extraordinarily productive career. From childhood appearances and record releases to a non-stop regimen of over half a century, he has produced an almost unparalleled catalogue of hits, a long list of exceptional tunes written for fellow musicians, many working within Motown, and a touring legacy that has taken him to locations around the globe where no Motown artist has previously gone. Winning virtually every award and accolade that the music industry has to offer, his humanitarian efforts on behalf of particularly challenged groups in society have been vast in scope, and steadfastly loyal.

As an experimental musician, Wonder gained at least competence, and usually a high degree of fluency, on so many instruments at a young age that he could, in many cases, man the recording studio single-handedly. Further, he was one of the pioneers in the modern studio, incorporating the Moog and other early synthesizers, along with a vast array of additional modern electronic instruments and effects, into his daily studio regimen. Never satisfied with merely passable skills in taking on any part of the creative process, he studied classical piano at the Michigan School for the Blind to improve his keyboard "chops" in every genre that he touched, despite never intending to appear on stage with Beethoven Sonatas or Chopin Etudes, more usual goals for such studies. By taking on this added level of skill, he developed not only the expected requirement of "covering" the correct notes, but took on a sensitive palette of touches, pedaling, and a fine-tuned sense for texture and quasi-vocal lines on keyboard instruments. Likewise, he studied traditionally classical and twentieth century music theory at the University of Southern California, one of the nation's premier classical music schools, to expand his harmonic and rhythmic language in the composition process.

As a result, Wonder possessed both the historical harmonic language of non-classical songwriting, and the advanced classical intricacies with which to create truly sophisticated, innovative examples, far beyond the normal keys, rhythms and harmonic progressions. These studies were all directed by an urge to become a world-leading musician and composer in every area of the studio, and Wonder ceaselessly "pushed to improve his musicianship and songwriting capabilities," maintaining a "deep commitment to his craft" throughout his career. His range of collaborations with fellow greats has taken him from duet work with the likes of rock giant Paul McCartney, to the exquisite songs of Barbara Streisand and the music of Broadway, and there is scarcely a nook within the popular market to which he has not contributed.

The Influential Legends of Soul Music: The Lives of Sam Cooke, Otis Redding, Marvin Gaye, Aretha Franklin, and Stevie Wonder looks at the lives and careers of some of America's most important musicians. Along with pictures of important people, places, and events, you will learn about these soul greats like never before.

The Influential Legends of Soul Music: The Lives of Sam Cooke, Otis Redding, Marvin Gaye, Aretha Franklin, and Stevie Wonder

About Charles River Editors

Introduction

Sam Cooke

   Chapter 1: Early Years with The Soul Stirrers

   Chapter 2: Secular Stardom

   Chapter 3: RCA

   Chapter 4: The Death of Sam Cooke

   Chapter 5: Sam Cooke's Legacy

Otis Redding

   Chapter 1: Early Years

   Chapter 2: The Beginning of Redding's Career

   Chapter 3: Stax

   Chapter 4: 1967

   Chapter 5: Redding's Death and the Aftermath

   Chapter 6: Redding's Legacy

Marvin Gaye

   Chapter 1: Troubled Childhood

   Chapter 2: Escape to Motown

   Chapter 3: Duets

   Chapter 4: What's Going On

   Chapter 5: At the Top?

   Chapter 6: Final Years

   Chapter 7: Marvin Gaye's Legacy

Aretha Franklin

   Chapter 1: Growing Up in Washington, D.C.

   Chapter 2: The Gospel Circuit

   Chapter 3: A Star In Her Own Right

   Chapter 4: The Queen

   Chapter 5: Career Challenges and Diva Status

   Chapter 6: Staying Power

Stevie Wonder

   Chapter 1: Childhood

   Chapter 2: Early Years at Motown

Chapter 3: Career Control
Chapter 4: Songs in the Key of Life
Chapter 5: The '80s
Chapter 6: The '90s
Chapter 7: Recent Years
Online Resources
Bibliography

Sam Cooke

Chapter 1: Early Years with The Soul Stirrers

Sam Cooke was born in the rural delta country of Clarksdale, Mississippi on January 22, 1931, an area in which social change moved more slowly than in the average American community, but he grew up in the city of Chicago after his father moved the family there during the Great Depression. As seemed to be the case with so many famous African-American singers and musicians, Cooke's father, Charles Cook, Sr., aspired to a position in the clergy, and in a mostly Baptist environment, he eventually succeeded. A Pentecostal, he became an assistant pastor at Christ Holiness Church, while working during the week as a domestic servant. Others refer to him as a "part-time preacher and Clarksdale oil mill worker."[14] Cooke's mother, Annie May, worked as a maid. Growing up in a family of eight children, with four brothers and three sisters, Cooke would later add the "e" to the end of his name.

The family's involvement in the church, where gospel lived and breathed on a weekly basis, was no brief Sunday morning regimen, as worship and preparation for worship took up the entire Sabbath, including the evening. Services began at 6:00 a.m. and continued through additional Bible study classes, extra services, and choir rehearsals. Added to that, the children formed a popular vocal ensemble called The Singing Children with Sam and his two sisters when he was nine.

It was while performing with this locally popular group that Cooke would be first seen and heard by J.W. Alexander, a noted tenor and manager for a gospel group known as the Pilgrim Travelers. More important for Cooke's later career, Alexander was an important talent scout for Specialty Records, a leading label for gospel music and most notably the home label for The Soul Stirrers, one of the most famous gospel ensembles in the business. The Soul Stirrers were formed by Roy Crain and enjoyed a career stretching to almost the span of a century in the jubilee style of gospel singing, a form of non-improvisational, close-harmony singing that began in academic circles but took on aspects of blues and jazz when it reached the black churches. Alexander had brought The Soul Stirrers and Specialty Records together in 1949 under the leadership of owner/president Art Rupe (born Arthur Goldberg in 1917), who had an extraordinary fondness for gospel music. Originally launching the label as Juke Box Records in 1946 in Los Angeles, Rupe was open to examples of rhythm & blues, blues, gospel, and early rock, even some of the more wild rhythm & blues examples that other labels might not have taken on, but he renamed the label to confirm to the market that he primarily specialized in African-American blues and gospel. Among Rupe's greatest prize of any genre was Little Richard, who signed with him in 1955, but barely two years later, Rupe ironically lost the star to a religious conversion.

---

[14] Mississippi Blues Trail, Sam Cooke – www.bluestrail.org/blues-trail-markers/sam-cooke

Little Richard

As if in a purposeful preparation for such an ensemble, Cooke took part in the establishment of a well-known gospel quintet called The Highway QCs, directly modeled after The Soul Stirrers and named for the Highway Baptist Church. Here, he sang with his brother, L.C. Cook, an avid singer and talented vocalist as well. Even in these years of seeming innocence, however, the urge toward secular music, a love of the attraction his voice evoked from audiences (especially girls), and the pursuit of profits had begun to come to the forefront. By his mid-teens, the change was clearly coming, and Cooke was "known to sneak into bars and sing for money for himself."[15] His pursuit of a lucrative solo career was never surreptitious, and according to his siblings, who observed that he "stood out in his ambitions,"[16] their brother stated openly and frequently, "I'm gonna sing and make a lot of money doing it."[17]

Two realities in Cooke's life made such a pronouncement possible. As a voracious student of

---

[15] Encyclopedia.com, Sam Cooke

[16] David Krajicek, Crime Library, the Death of Sam Cooke – www.crimelibrary.com/notorious_murders/celebrity/Sam_Cooke/13.html

[17] David Krajicek, Crime Library

investing, he was able to become an "astute, independent-minded businessman,"[18] Cooke had an affinity for the ladies as well, and it certainly helped that he had the type of voice, according to his brother, that could "charm the birds out of the trees."[19] Professional and personal support were never far away, and the secular life seemed, despite his family's wishes, to be unavoidable. Not only was he totally preoccupied with the desire to sing, he "could think of no other vocation for himself."[20] In retrospect, some observers assert that even then, it was clear that Cooke viewed his life as a gospel singer "as simply an apprenticeship to the secular world."[21]

Cooke's entrance into both the worldly and spiritual professional worlds brought wildly disparate results. Upon his graduation from Wendell Phillips High School in 1948, where one of his idols, the great Nat King Cole, was an alum, and where Cooke had made his mark as an excellent student (being voted most likely to succeed by his class), he was invited to join The Soul Stirrers as their lead singer in 1948, replacing R.H. Harris, the group's "legendary lead singer."[22] This was the dream of a lifetime to Cooke, and a particularly distinguished honor to anyone who knew anything about the gospel world at the time. The Soul Stirrers were among the elite and most widely known of the great gospel ensembles, "one of the top acts on the all night Gospel circuit."[23]

---

[18] David Krajicek, Crime Library

[19] Peter Guralnick, Dream Boogie, p. 98

[20] Peter Guralnick, Dream Boogie, p. 98

[21] David Wolf, "You Send Me: the Life and Times of Sam Cooke – He Gave Us Water" Review by Darryl Cox, in the Threepenny Review, No. 67, Autumn, 1996

[22] IMDb Sam Cooke Biography – www.imdb.com/name/nm1077492/bio?ref_=nm_ov_bio_sm

[23] History of Rock, Sam Cooke – www.history-of-rock.com/cooke.htm

Nat King Cole

Immediately presented with five new suits, Cooke went on to perform over a thousand concerts with the Soul Stirrers in a period of six years, and in one 12 month period alone, the group logged over 100,000 miles on the road. In addition to his vocal qualities, Cooke became known for his masterful vocal diction, which was almost as distinctive as his voice. R.H. Harris claimed responsibility for teaching Cooke this art, an idea at which the new star simply laughed. According to those in and closest to the group, Cooke's diction had been superior to Harris' from the start.

However, contradictions between Cooke's spiritual profession and his private behavior would soon begin to cause problems. During the same month in which Cooke was invited to join The Soul Stirrers fresh out of high school, he was arrested on a morals charge for delivering pornographic material to an acquaintance. For this, he spent three months in the Cook County Jail. In this first case of his private flaws working against his career pursuits, Cooke survived the scandal, and amazingly enough, his charmed life in the gospel world was not ultimately undermined either, allowing his "meteoric rise"[24] to continue. Able to put it behind him for the moment, he carried sufficient clout in the gospel world to remain a major artist and create a number of hits by the middle of the '50s. With such repeated behavior, however, preserving a clean image became increasingly difficult with his newfound fame. The world of religious artists was far from being scandal-free, but Cooke began to take on the role of gospel's "bad-boy" with each passing incident.

Furthermore, Cooke's style of performance and vocal sound created a persistent (albeit subconscious) undercurrent among The Soul Stirrers' audience that his vocal charms were not entirely non-secular in the gospel realm. His was a voice that could be picked out of a thousand, a "distinctive tenor, [with a] unique shivery way of hitting the high notes."[25] This "shivery" quality, among his many other vocal assets, infused a feeling of secular romance into pure gospel. Some recognized it as such, while others simply perceived it as a higher, holier level of artistic expression. Famous soul crooner Tom Wilson, however, caught the feeling that Cooke was not evoking something altogether spiritual, recognizing the thin boundary between religion and seduction: "Them sisters fell like dominoes when Sam took the lead."[26] Gospel writer Joe McEwen described it in a similarly forthright way by observing that Cooke "never sang songs that were more erotic and buoyant than the love songs he sang about his Lord."[27]

The natural condition of Cooke's voice fit the role of the perfect crooner, and it was entirely against his nature and physicality to be a shouter, as was popular in many parts of both the spiritual and secular musical communities. Following his best instincts, which included highly sensitive phrasing and pure vocal timbre, "he sang his spirituals with intimacy,"[28] the very basis by which to establish a hybrid secular form and a romantic sense of intimacy applied to any heavenly or earthly subject. Cooke's "light, lilting vocal style that soared rather than thundered"[29] could be taken anywhere, into any sort of music, in the same way that Marian Anderson had applied the smoothness and richness of her voice to spirituals, then to German Lieder and back again, or the precious sound that McCormack used for either the Ave Maria or romantic Irish ballads. Such a tradition was not new to Cooke, but in the emergence of a new form, gospel purists were both caught off-guard and simultaneously thrilled by the sensual aspects of Cooke's vocal persona. In one critic's politest terms, Cooke's voice and delivery was "a potent stimulant."[30]

By 1955, Cooke had achieved several major hits in the gospel market, which was a

---

[24] IMDb, Sam Cooke Biography
[25] James Nadal, All About Jazz
[26] Encyclopedia.com, Sam Cooke
[27] Encyclopedia.com, Sam Cooke
[28] Peter Guralnick, Boogie Dreams, p. 98
[29] Peter Guralnick, Boogie Dreams, p. 98
[30] Peter Guralnick, Boogie Dreams, p.98

considerably smaller niche than the secular industries. These included "Jesus, Wash Away My Troubles," and "Touch the Hem of His Garment." Aretha Franklin, a younger singer who would go on to have a significant professional interaction with Cooke, referred to these and other examples as "perfectly chiseled jewels."[31] Among other live appearances, Cooke would sing in R.C. Franklin's (Aretha's father) church in Detroit on more than one occasion. In addition, he did a fair amount of radio work, including broadcasts over the Memphis all-black station, WDIA. This forum, established in 1947 by white owners John Pepper and Dick Ferguson, offered a weekly show for black artists but took off commercially when they went all black, elevating them to the city's premier station. WDIA served as a tremendous boost for the launching of African-American careers, was one of the most influential black radio stations in the South, and became the first of its kind in the United States.

Aretha Franklin

In the waning days of Cooke's tenure with The Soul Stirrers, he took a stand that few were willing to take at the time, including fellow members of the ensemble, by refusing to perform before a segregated audience. It was an almost unheard of gesture, and an attack on the entire Southern system of segregation. The first distinct sign and "first real effort[s] at civil disobedience,"[32] it would not be his last, with musical statements on the social conditions in America remaining to be made, in tandem with similar diatribes musically expressed by great American white artists like Bob Dylan. At the time, this was a step almost nobody was willing to

---

[31] David Ritz, Encyclopaedia Britannica
[32] IMDb, Sam Cooke Biography

take, but Cooke's flat refusal moved progress along, however slowly, toward integrated audiences.

Cooke's first official step into the world of soul music, the new hybrid form that brought elements of gospel into the secular world, began and almost ended within the studios of Specialty Records. Specializing in gospel, and having been established in the '40s by Arthur Rupe, Specialty Records fairly owned The Soul Stirrers, and the studio had provided a great deal of Cooke's success thus far. Thus, his unfortunate collision with prevailing norms came in a couple of forms when the executive walked in unannounced on a recording session. Cooke was recording a love song entitled "Lovable," a remake of "Wonderful," in a studio that stood for the gospel industry, and he was covering George Gershwin's "Summertime" from the folk opera "Porgy and Bess" (eventually intended to serve as a B side). Rupe was furious on both counts, and there was one more fundamental point of disagreement between Rupe, Cooke, and Bumps Blackwell, bandleader, writer (of the later hit "You Send Me"), producer, arranger, and the one in charge of the session. Rupe had expected Cooke to be more of a shouter along the lines of Little Richard, who was already in the Specialty stable, so when he was confronted with such an intimate, refined vocal style and such a contrary repertoire to the Specialty mission, Rupe was "quite upset."[33] Blackwell was immediately fired after a lengthy argument, and Cooke was replaced on the Specialty roster by a young performer named Sonny Bono who was still in search of his first break. In the same way that Rupe would lose Little Richard to religion, he would lose Sam Cooke to the allure of pop music, with his presence as a member of The Soul Stirrers continuing to cause problems in the public arena. It is said that Rupe, perhaps in part from these transitions, "lost interest in making records"[34] over time. Some years later, the label would be sold to Fantasy Records and is now part of SONY/ATV.

Other artists in other genres had attempted the practice of crossing over by changing styles and using various aliases, often with great success. In the music industry of the '50s, however, the sacred and profane between black gospel and pop music were kept apart with great vehemence. The purity of gospel music was sacrosanct within the African-American community, and "constraints against gospel performers performing secular material were strong and woven deep into the fabric of the black community."[35] When Cooke's secular offering reached awaiting ears outside the studio, everyone knew the real singer's identity at once, even though he had released the song under the name of Dale Cook. In releasing "Lovable," a grievous breach of good faith had been committed, and The Soul Stirrers, accustomed to sitting at the top of their industry, were actually booed at some of their performances, which would have been previously unthinkable.

Given the condition of such rigid separation between faith and the world, there would be no

---

[33] Shaw Star.com, Sam Cooke Biography – www.shawstar.com/music/sam-cooke.htm

[34] Concord Music Group, Specialty Records – www.concordmusicgroup.com/labels/Specialty

[35] History of Rock, Sam Cooke

chance at reconciliation, compromise or coexistence. Such a public offering could not exist in parallel with a continued gospel career, especially within such a famous group. As a result, Rupe dropped Cooke for "deserting The Soul Stirrers" and replaced him with Johnny Taylor.

Chapter 2: Secular Stardom

Cooke in *Billboard Magazine*

Now out of The Soul Stirrers, the line had been crossed for Cooke, and he had no choice but to pursue a secular career as best he could, which had almost always been his deepest desire anyway. While it was true that the non-gospel market offered a great deal more in terms of income, there were no guarantees that Cooke would survive in the finicky world of pop singing, where a performer can be in or out of fashion in a moment despite great vocal gifts. For the next few months, Cooke allowed the emotional temperature over the Specialty Records flap to cool; there would be no releases of any kind, of any genre, under either his name or any other, and the young artist with the rare voice seemed unable, at first, to create the new connections necessary to re-inventing himself.

In quite another way, the timing could not have been more fortuitous. By the late '50s, Cooke had observed, as had many others, that the gospel industry was losing ground as a commercial market, and among all the other secular forms, Rhythm & Blues was perceived by many, even the religious, as "a less threatening hybrid of several black music traditions."[36] Opinions and moral judgments varied as Cooke made the change from gospel to soul, but some of the reactions closest to home were surprisingly moderate, even at home. Charles Cook, Sr., despite his deep religious commitment and position within the church, expressed a belief that in his son's case, what he sang was actually less important. What he did stress as important was that "God gave you a good voice to use. He must want you to make people happy by singing, so go ahead and do so."[37]

Whatever the personal feelings toward Cooke's transformation, almost everyone initially advised against the move as a purely practical matter. As a gospel artist, with either The Soul Stirrers or as a solo artist, he was an ace, and there was no denying it. According to historian Tony Heilbut, Cooke was simply "the greatest sex symbol in gospel history,"[38] further describing him as "a sort of holy heart-throb."[39] However, when Cooke made the decision to move on, he made it without reservation or timidity. Leaving behind every vestige of his former self, professionally at least, he replaced the trappings of his gospel-oriented life with uncharacteristically non-religious symbols. As one writer noted, Cooke "not only left the church, [and] gospel, [but he] started [his] own secular label, [and] invested in a beer company, 'Cooke's Beer.'"[40]

Much of Cooke's transformation took place during the year of 1957, and despite the tenuous nature of making it in popular music, he became an almost instant success. Considering his artistic and physical assets, Cooke's natural advantages greatly increased the chance of such immediate recognition. As he had in the gospel world, Cooke's vocal allure drew new listeners in with his simply-delivered perfection, "never pushing or straining his voice, no flailing,

[36] James Nadal, All About Jazz
[37] ABKO, Artists, Sam Cooke – www.abko.com/index.php/artists/artist/16/sam-cooke
[38] David W. Cloud, Adherents.com, Home Page, the Religious Affiliation of Rock and Roll Legend Sam Cooke – www.adherents.com/people/pc/Sam_Cooke.html
[39] David W. Cloud, Adherents
[40] David W. Cloud, Adherents

cathartic vocal runs, no bursts of horns, just precious filigree…"[41] By the age of 20, he had already perfected the technique of his "hypnotically smooth voice…a finely-honed instrument."[42] Along with his "finely chiseled good looks"[43] a well-cultivated "twinkle in the eye for the ladies"[44] (one which seemed to meet with constant reciprocation), and his astute sense of social manners, Cooke was finally able to "reinvent himself as a romantic crooner in the manner of Nat King Cole."[45] In the end, the resulting attraction between listener and artist was the same as it had been in the gospel world, with the added rewards of a larger market in pop music and far wider latitude in artistic content. Bringing the best of what had made him so irresistible to sacred music audiences, he "brought a gospel authority to pop songs about broken hearts and puppy love."[46]

In the same year, Cooke signed on to the William Morris Agency in California and appeared on television broadcasts such as *The Guy Mitchell Show*, a short-lived but popular variety venue at the time. In accordance with the prevailing custom, Cooke devoted himself almost entirely to the recording and releasing of what he hoped would become hit singles, as the album was not yet a record-buyer's concept. By 1957, and over the following two years, Cooke went right to work, recording a number of upbeat songs in blues style. Stylistically and vocally, he reflected a great deal of influence from one of his early idols, "the melodious, harmony-based sounds of the Ink Spots."[47] Not all of the examples were destined for "hit" status, but they reflected an important time of preparation for later, more weighty releases. Such bluesy singles included "Little Red Rooster," "Somebody Have Mercy," George Gershwin's "Summertime," "Frankie and Johnny," "Laughin' and Clownin'," "Only Sixteen," "Everybody Loves to Cha Cha," and "Sad Mood."

"Only Sixteen," one of the more successful attempts, was written by Lou Adler, but it was submitted instead as having been written by Barbara Campbell, one of Cooke's many girlfriends and the one he would eventually marry. This avoided legal burdens by negating any peripheral claims to royalty payments or conditions of ownership. "You Send Me," for Keen Records, a vastly more lucrative hit and the biggest thus far, was written by Bumps Blackwell, and like later examples, would be orchestrated and conducted by René Hall. The B-side to "You Send Me" was Gershwin's "Summertime." Cooke had originally given the song to his brother L.C. and hoped that he would record it instead, but L.C. was never able to make a good go of it.

An early attempt at assembling an album, based on the work of Billie Holiday, came out in 1959 and was entitled "Tribute to the Lady." Despite the brilliance of the material, it never caught on in the long run, and its failure to do so is still debated. Whether it was the concept of an album, the subject chosen, the songs' affinity for Cooke's brand of performance, the

---

[41] Jacob Ganz, NPR Music, The Record, Sam Cooke at 80: The Career that Could have Been, Jan. 21, 2011

[42] IMDb, Sam Cooke Biography

[43] IMDb, Sam Cooke Biography

[44] David Krajicek, Crime Library

[45] David Ritz, Encyclopaedia Britannica

[46] Jacob Ganz, NPR Music

[47] Bruce Eder, MSN Entertainment, Sam Cooke Biography – www.msn.com/music/artist-biography/sam-cooke/

packaging, or any other number of possibilities, "Tribute" did somewhat well at first but then suddenly vanished from the charts.

Billie Holiday

Compensating for the lack of success on the album front, the first enormous hit single that came from Cooke's early years was "You Send Me," which shot to number one on all of the charts and held its popularity for over four months. By the end of the year, "You Send Me" knocked Elvis Presley's "Jailhouse Rock" from the top positions across the board and went on to spend the next 26 weeks in the top spot. All told, 1.7 million copies were sold.

From this point on, life would obviously change, and Cooke found himself able to go places where black artists could not generally go, including to venues such as the prestigious Copacabana in New York, "previously off-limits to Rhythm & Blues acts."[48] Despite breaking new ground with such appearances, it did not work out particularly well for Cooke's core following, and the authentic spirit of the artist was not demonstrated before an appreciative but older white audience. Essentially playing for the parents of his white following, Cooke chose his least threatening, most mainstream repertoire, and he presented himself to the upscale New Yorkers "at his most congenial."[49] He was politely accepted, even well-liked by the audience, but the Copa clientele applauded him for his "tamest persona."[50]

1958 did not go as easily as it might have for Cooke. His early marriage to Dee Dee (Delores) Mohawk, a singer from Texas, had ended, and she died soon after in an automobile accident by striking a tree while drunk. Within a short time of that occurrence, Cooke had his own serious automobile accident, one that put friend and colleague Lou Rawls in the hospital with serious injuries.

[48] David Ritz, Encyclopaedia Britannica
[49] Bruce Eder, MSN Entertainment
[50] Bruce Eder, MSN Entertainment

A picture from the Orange County Archives of Lou Rawls and Frank Gorshin

Cooke was engaged to make his first appearance on *The Ed Sullivan Show* in March of 1958, but due to unexpected time constraints, his performance was cut off before he had scarcely begun, much to the chagrin of the famous host. Only able to lip-sync a fragment of "You Send Me" before the interruption, Sullivan apologized profusely and rescheduled Cooke's appearance. It was fortunate that "You Send Me" remained atop the charts for so long, and that other hits began to emerge, or else Cooke might not have had anything important to bring to the rescheduled appearance.

However, the most difficult aspect of 1958 was made possible by Cooke's sudden success, and by his oldest and most destructive flaw. With an already legendary charm to go along with his status as a star, the year "arrived with an unexpected adjunct; paternity lawsuits,"[51] most of

---

[51] David Krajicek, Crime Library

which he was able to settle out of court. In a fit of jealousy that came at a time in which his off-and-on girlfriend, Barbara Campbell, was about to marry a Baptist minister, Cooke rushed to her residence and persuaded her to marry him instead. The wedding was held at his grandmother's home, with his father presiding. In retrospect, Barbara's decision to marry a minister might have been fraught with marital peril, but it's fair to wonder how much better it was for her to be with Sam Cooke. The two already had children together (daughters Linda and Tracey), but while Cooke "calculated an image of urbanity while admiring the street life,"[52] not to mention a flagrant history of continuing infidelity, Barbara, to the contrary, "had no such pretentions, taking up with pimps and drug dealers."[53] Whether Barbara shared his roving eye, or whether she had simply had enough at one point, she went on to entertain a number of affairs as well. With Barbara, his high school sweetheart, Cooke would have three children in all.

Employing his accumulated business smarts, which were prodigious for having spent such a short time in the industry, Cooke established a record and publishing company in 1959, of which the recording component would go through various names, including SAR and Tracey Records (named after one of his daughters). A business venture designed to further the work of others, Cooke did not use it for his own releases; in fact, one of the first acts signed by the fledgling label was none other than The Soul Stirrers, including the man who had replaced him, Johnny Taylor.

That same year, Cooke signed with Keen Records, established by Bob Keane, after Blackwell had received Cooke's contract from Art Rupe in lieu of royalty payments from Specialty Records. Bob Keane was a clarinetist and former leader of the Artie Shaw Band, and although his was not one of the larger labels, it was one that granted a certain of amount of latitude when it came to artistic vision. In order to prevent legal incursions on Cooke's biggest hit, "You Send Me," Keane and Cooke maintained that the song had been composed by Cooke's brother, L.C., escaping any peripheral claims by Specialty Records. Following that, they proceeded to make a literal fortune with the single, free of external payments. During a frenzied regimen of recording that year, Cooke produced a string of similar love songs, all of them underpinned with "pretty arrangements and sung with a rolling, medium tempo."[54]

Chapter 3: RCA

By 1960, however, trouble had already started at Keen. Cooke and Bob Keane parted company over a royalty dispute, and for a short time, Cooke concentrated solely on the success of his business venture. Not yet a high profile label, its prestige nevertheless began to grow as Cooke insisted on using the best musicians in Los Angeles and monitored all the important details with precision and good judgment. Still pursuing a legal suit against Keen as the new decade began,

---

[52] Peter Guralnick, Dream Boogie, p. 98

[53] Peter Guralnick, Dream Boogie p. 98

[54] History of Rock, Sam Cooke

Cooke struck one of the most impressive bargains imaginable with the prestigious RCA Records, which was incredibly impressive and unheard of for an African-American artist. The deal of deals reached with RCA included a sizeable advance, and a promise that following a 30 period, all rights of ownership pertaining to masters of all recordings would default to Cooke. Theoretically, assuming that at least some of those hits would enjoy an iconic and enduring longevity, Cooke would come into ownership of his best work around the age of 60. Furthermore, all business transactions were channeled, when possible, through his own label, and by means of this procedural arrangement, Cooke helped to advance the careers of such artists as Bobby Womack, Billy Preston, and others.

Bill Ebbesen's picture of Bobby Womack

In a further stroke of good luck, Cooke was eventually successful in the suit against Keen and won a sizeable settlement, thereby "bankrupting the label."[55] However, despite the tremendous burden on the former company, Keen was able to release Cooke's latest hit, "Wonderful World," an enigmatic song written by Lou Adler and Herb Alpert. Neither of the writers thought that the quirky piece would ever amount to anything and believed it to be trivial at best, but it was Cooke himself who continually drew their attention back to it, despite the composers' misgivings. Taken from the last recording session with Keen, "Wonderful World" sold over a million copies and at least partially saved the day for Bob Keane.

---

[55] Peter Guralnick, Boogie Dreams, p. 98

At the time in which he moved to RCA, Cooke was a highly sought-after artist, and one of the first two black artists, along with Harry Belafonte, to ever sign with the label, but when he was originally unhappy with the arrangement, Cooke formed KAGS Music in an attempt to control the destiny of his own music. At RCA, his work adopted a "grittier, more gospel-influenced feel,"[56] but RCA would forestall other releases, believing that certain examples were too raw and rough-edged for the time. Perhaps one of the more successful releases of Cooke's early RCA involvement was "Chain Gang," a curious choice of subject matter for the record-buying audience and a song laced with interesting sound effects to approximate the clanking of chains. Cooke actually paid a visit to get a feel for the real thing.

Belafonte

It's rare for a new artist's first efforts with an unfamiliar record company to become a hit, and generally speaking, the studio needs time to find the best fits for the music, packaging, and

---

[56] Classic Bands.com, Sam Cooke – www.classicbands.com/cooke.html

promotion. Cooke's first major recording project with RCA was no exception, to the extent that it did badly by any conceivable measuring stick, even though "Teenage Sonata" had been set up to be a "sure smash."[57] Both Cooke and the studio had high hopes for the release, and promotion included full-page ads in all of the most important trade magazines. In the aftermath, the highest that "Teenage Sonata" would ever climb was #50 before it disappeared immediately afterward.

RCA did scarcely better with the highly-trumpeted "Hits of the Fifties" and "Cooke's Tour." Again released with high expectations, these offerings barely created any stir at all among the record-buying public and fizzled shortly after being introduced. The critics were even less kind, with one saying that "Hits" was probably the "lamest LP ever recorded by any Soul or R&B singer."[58] To accompany that note of finality, the review continued to address the album as consisting of nothing other than "washed out pop tunes."[59] Clearly, RCA had not yet found the recipe for success with its new star.

Not everything went amiss, however. In 1960, "Nobody Loves Me Like You" became a big hit for The Flamingos, and even though record sales for Cooke were not yet finding the mark, his live tours were successful beyond expectations, and he spent the month of March performing for full houses throughout the Caribbean. The touring regimen was almost incessant during the early '60s, and much of it was spent working with then 18 year old Aretha Franklin. In his continuing efforts with RCA, his own record company's work also continued, not only as a way to advance the careers of artists like the Simms Twins, Bobby Womack, and Johnny Taylor, but also as a way to keep control of the flow of money from Cooke's releases. In the same year, the Keen release of "Wonderful World," to the surprise of almost everyone who had ever worked on it, helped to sustain Cooke's flow of hits, propping up his fortunes in addition to staving off the inevitable for the label.

Among the highlights of 1961 were four recordings, including "Cupid," which is now considered a classic despite bringing in only moderate sales. Meanwhile, the 1962 dance track "Twistin' the Night Away" did well as a throwback to the earlier, more flip examples of Cooke's early work with Keen, and during the same year, Cooke teamed up again with friend Lou Rawls on the old gospel song "Bring it on Back to Me." As his musical reputation grew, so did Cooke's status as a tabloid target. In 1962, a rumor gained traction that Cooke had developed leukemia, would die imminently, and had promised to donate his eyes to Ray Charles, an entirely unfounded idea. For the gossip industry, Cooke was a dream come true: beautiful voice, good looks, and a sordid past to match.

[57] Michael Jack Kirby, Way Back Attack, Sam Cooke – www.waybackattack.com/cookesam.html
[58] Bruce Eder, MSU Entertainment
[59] Bruce Eder, MSU Entertainment

Sam Cooke in the studio in 1961

Soon after, RCA released "The Best of Sam Cooke," containing many of the best hits recorded between 1957 and 1962, including those recorded at other studios. Following that was the odd intimacy of "Another Saturday Night," a tongue-in-cheek account of a single man "stuck on a date with a girl who had a strange resemblance to a cat named Frankenstein."[60] It was an uncharacteristic release, considering the body of work being produced in this part of the decade.

In 1963, Cooke was touring England with Little Richard, and in a new deal with RCA, all business was re-routed through Tracey Records, Cooke's company, which meant that by that

---

[60] Michael Jack Kirby, Way Back Attack

time, RCA was reduced to the role of distributor. From that deal, and from past arrangements, RCA had within the past three years advanced Cooke half a million dollars, an enormous sum for the decade and for an artist of his race. Cooke also began to keep a high-profile level of company by the early part of the decade, including attending the first historic bout between Cassius Clay and Sonny Liston with Malcolm X. Cooke also later produced Muhammad Ali's recording of "The Gang's All Here" as the boxer became a star himself.

In Miami's Harlem Square, Sam Cooke delivered a performance which most historians consider one of the best ever offered in his style of music. It was a more aggressive, rough, and thought-provoking Cooke that appeared that night, the exact opposite of the placid personality he had shown to the audiences at the Copacabana. RCA, however, was rattled by the tone of the performance and chose not to release it for another 22 years, perhaps fearing that during the Civil Rights Movement, such daring on stage might evoke an overreaction. One can only wonder what might have been had RCA gone ahead and released "Harlem Square," one of Cooke's most riveting performances, but for the company, the danger was such that a backlash might cause the loss of profits and institutional reputation. As an RCA executive, Greg Geller, later put it, "Sam was what we've come to call a crossover artist: He crossed over from gospel to pop, which was controversial enough in its day. But once he became a pop artist, he had a certain mainstream image to protect. The fact is, when he was out on the road, he was playing to a predominantly, almost exclusively black audience. And he was doing a different kind of show — a much more down-home, down-to-earth, gut-bucket kind of show than what he would do for his pop audience." Another music critic noted, "Not only is this one of the greatest live soul albums ever released, it also reveals a rougher, rawer, and more immediate side to Sam Cooke that his singles only hinted at, good as they were… the crucial key is and was always Cooke's vocals, and while he was a marvelously smooth, versatile, and urbane singer on his official pop recordings, here he explodes into one of the finest sets of raw secular gospel ever captured on tape. It is essential listening in any version."

As if destiny would not let go of the point, Cooke and his band were turned away from a Holiday Inn in Shreveport, Louisiana, clearly on racial grounds and not from lack of space. In the same way that Cooke had refused to sing before a segregated audience years before, on this night he refused to leave the premises, despite Barbara's objections that someone was bound to kill him if he made too many waves. Brushing it all off, he attempted to comfort her by saying they wouldn't hurt him because he was Sam Cooke, but she insisted, "To them, you're just another…you know."[61] In the end, Cooke left the grounds, but he was still arrested for disturbing the peace with his colleagues.

Understandably chafing over such experiences, once he was home, Cooke went back into the studio to create a substantive musical commentary that would serve as an African-American

---

[61] NPR Music, NPR staff, Feb. 1, 2014, Sam Cooke and the Song That Almost Scared Him – www.npr.org/2014/02/01/268995033/sam-cooke-and-the-song-that-almost-scared-him

statement to be put forward in parallel with similar releases of Bob Dylan and other members of the protest movement. He had always wished that a black artist would come up with something equally powerful to Dylan's social masterpiece "Blowin' In The Wind," and the Shreveport incident provided the spark. A month later, he emerged with "A Change is Gonna Come," taken from a blend of inspirations, including the hotel rejection, Dylan's "Blowin' In The Wind," the Martin Luther King march in Memphis, and other personal experiences from Memphis, Shreveport, and Birmingham.

As his colleagues recalled it, Cooke became "a bit of a control freak"[62] in the studio, and the only exception involved his wish for the piece to be epic in nature. As part of the scope of the social statement, he wanted the song to possess a sense of grandeur, and indeed, each section is dominated by an edificial orchestral section, one with strings and another with horns. The bridge is taken by the timpani. Cooke, uncharacteristic of the process in which this track was recorded, placed an implicit trust in arranger René Hall, who also conducted on the recording. The two had worked together before, and they went all out on the orchestration, employing 17 strings all in all for the final product.

"A Change is Gonna Come" was released in March 1964 after being previewed by former Specialty Records member J.W. Alexander, a singer, musician, songwriter, producer and entrepreneur who had sung as a member of The Soul Stirrers. The release was part of the album "Ain't That Good News," and once finished, he asked fellow artist Bobby Womack to offer an opinion on the song. Clearly, Womack was not quite ready to make a statement of such magnitude on a public stage, and he responded that the song "sounds like death…that's why I'm never playing it in public."[63] Cooke, not dissuaded, went ahead with the release and live performances, challenging those venues who feared it, but he would not live long enough to see the album officially released.

In a subsequent performance, Cooke re-emphasized his civil rights statement by performing Dylan's "Blowin' in the Wind," though it is unknown precisely how the chosen setting of the performance came about. It was probably the first and only time in which Dylan's classic was performed with go-go dancers in the background, and it is difficult to believe that Cooke himself choreographed it that way, feeling as he did about the song and its implications.

Chapter 4: The Death of Sam Cooke

"It's been too hard living, but I'm afraid to die. Cause I don't know what's up there beyond the sky"

Even before his tragic death, 1964 was a difficult one for Sam Cooke. Cooke and his family suffered a tragic loss when their son, Vincent, drowned in the pool at the Cooke residence at

---

[62] NPR Music
[63] NPR Music

barely two years of age. Alongside his personal loss, professional resistance to his socially conscious music continued; appearing on *The Tonight Show with Johnny Carson* in that year, the staff pressured him to perform something other than "A Change is Gonna Come," but he insisted. Following that appearance, however, he never performed the song live in public again, partly due to the high difficulty and instrumental requirements of the arrangement. The album, "Ain't That Good News," came out with five hit singles, despite only modest sales as an album, and "A Change is Gonna Come" remained a controversial issue wherever Cooke went. In fact, on the version that was released as a single, one line was edited out: "I go to the movie and I go downtown, somebody keep tellin' me don't hang around." In an era when most other artists were still singing about village love and obeying the racial guidelines set forth by the music industry, Cooke had worked tirelessly to put together a crossover career after sacrificing an early one, and this particular offering didn't fit well into either one of them. It was one thing for Dylan or Baez to confront the social structure head-on, but no one expected an African-American soul singer to catch the protest fever and "address social problems in [such] a direct and explicit way."[64] The last thing Cooke wanted was to offend the core of his audience, but he felt taken over by the moral outrage that had preoccupied him during his gospel days, and he let the song go forward. Long after his death, "A Change is Gonna Come" remains his signature song, and despite the controversy of the moment, he still occupied a high position in the industry, with offices in the Warner Brothers Building in Hollywood and a lovely house on Ames Street in Los Feliz. While a shocking civil rights movement or anti-war release may have been fine for Bob Dylan, such a move could put Cooke's now comfortable life at considerable risk.

Meanwhile, in March 1964, Cooke's hits from the Copacabana were released by RCA on a live album, featuring the classics from an older generation he had performed for the more stolid audience there. The release included songs such as "The Best Things in Life are Free," "Bill Bailey," "Nobody Knows You When You're Down and Out," "If I Had a Hammer," "This Little Light of Mine," and the revered "Tennessee Waltz," basically white or non-race specific content written decades earlier.

The direction in which Sam Cooke's career would've gone after 1964 is one of music history's greatest what-ifs, because the great singer was killed on December 11, 1964, a month shy of his 34th birthday, after a strange chain of events that culminated in what has been described as "one of the greatest tragedies in the history of popular music."[65] Indeed, the various accounts of Cooke's death differ wildly, as supporters wish to present him in a more pristine light and detractors attempt to tear away all signs of glamour in discussing the young star. In the middle are many procedural questions directed at both the police and the court, and a raft of suspicious accounts and unanswered questions as to what really took place. Given such a tangled report of what truly occurred, biographer Peter Guralnick nevertheless maintains that "there is not a single

---

[64] NPR Music

[65] Rolling Stone, Happy Belated Birthday to the Great Sam Cooke – www.rollingstone.com/music/news/happy-belated-80th-birthday-to-the-great-sam-cooke-20110124

person that believes that Sam Cooke died as he is said to have died."[66]

Whatever the details, the night of Cooke's death seemingly started with a recurrence of his most notorious flaw, one of "Biblical proportions, his unbridled libido."[67] From the beginning, Cooke had been susceptible to advances from adoring female fans and had a special affinity for the less complicated relationships he could have with prostitutes. In fact, Cooke's friend and producer, Bumps Blackwell, had always maintained that "Sam would walk past a good girl to get to a whore,"[68] if only because a good girl was too much trouble. Despite the fact that Barbara would greet the news of her husband's death with hysterics, his ongoing infidelity was not much of a shock to her; during their time together, he had "juggled three pregnant girlfriends, two in Chicago, one in Cleveland"[69] at the same time. As a "skirt chaser and serial philanderer,"[70] his extramarital partners had given birth to three daughters in a five-week period.

According to colleague Ike Turner, who claimed to possess a special knowledge of the incident, Cooke had just withdrawn a sizeable amount of money for the purchase of Christmas presents and was drinking at Martoni's Restaurant in Los Angeles with producer Al Schmitt and his wife Joan. According to those present, Cooke had three or four martinis and made no attempt to hide his wad of bills to restaurant patrons. Excusing himself, he was later found "cozied up in a booth"[71] with a young woman named Elisa Boyer, described as a "baby-faced twenty-two year old Asian girl"[72] of mixed European descent. Reportedly a woman of questionable background herself, it is unknown which of the two initiated the decision to go elsewhere; some report that she was a regular hooker, and others claim that Boyer and Cooke had dated in the past. According to Turner, whose source remains unknown, Boyer was known in the area as a "drunk roller"[73] whose modus operandi was to steal money from "johns" after getting them drunk, and if necessary, knocking them unconscious when they relaxed their guard. Boyer had apparently witnessed Cooke flashing his large roll of bills but was not aware at the time that he was a celebrity of any sort.

Whatever the circumstances, Cooke and Boyer left the restaurant together and drove away in his Ferrari before ending up in a cheap motel called the Hacienda, where Bertha Franklin served as the night manager. Boyer later claimed that she had insisted Cooke take her home, and she reported to police that she was the victim of an attempted rape and kidnapping. Boyer allegedly left the room while Cooke was in the bathroom, taking her clothes and most of his with her before phoning the police from another location. However, in his writings and national radio

---

[66] Peter Guralnick, Boogie Dreams

[67] David Krajicek, Crime Library

[68] Lydia Hutchinson, Performing Songwriter, the Mysterious Death of Sam Cooke – www.performingsongwriter.com/mysterious-death-sam-cooke/

[69] David Krajicek, Crime Library

[70] David Krajicek, Crime Library

[71] Lydia Hutchinson, Performing Songwriter

[72] Lydia Hutchinson, Performing Songwriter

[73] IMDb, Sam Cooke Biography

interviews, Peter Guralnick, Cooke's primary biographer, is vehement in separating Cooke the philanderer from Cooke the alleged bully, claiming that it was not in the singer's nature to commit the kind of aggression Boyer had claimed. Guralnick explained, "I can't imagine him attacking her. He wasn't that type of person…you never heard of Sam Cooke beating up his women."[74] Furthermore, Ike Turner claimed that a large amount of Cooke's cash went with her, and a certain sum was reported as missing, with its whereabouts still unknown.

Whether Sam Cooke eventually came to from a blow on the head, or whether he simply returned from the bathroom, it is reported that he assembled what clothes he could, which included a suit coat and little else, and went to the manager's office on the site. There is no one to counter Bertha Franklin's charge that Cooke was in a belligerent state, and it was a well-known fact that the singer had an "explosive temper."[75] According to Franklin, Cooke lunged at the door, shouting at her to tell him the whereabouts of the girl before finally knocking the door down. When Franklin's response was not immediately forthcoming, he grabbed and began to wrestle with her, resulting in both of them falling to the floor. She would later tell police that "he fell on top of me. I tried to bite him…scratching and everything…got up…kicked him. I run and grabbed the pistol off the TV, and I shot at close range, three times."[76] Conversely, Ike Turner's account, which has always been impossible to verify, claimed that Cooke ran to the office, where he witnessed Franklin and Boyer at the desk counting out his money. In line with that theory, it was believed by many that Boyer and Franklin knew each other and were working together to profit off of unwary "johns."

According to Franklin's account, Cooke got up from the floor after being shot three times and spoke his last words: "Lady, you shot me!"[77] It was then that she began to hit him over the head with a broom handle until he fell again and was silent. The final report indicated that Franklin was in possession of a .32 caliber handgun, but that she had killed Cooke with a .22. When officers arrived, they found Cooke's Ferrari in the parking lot with one door open, a bottle of Scotch in the front seat, and the engine running.

Following a series of death threats directed against Franklin, she lost her job shortly afterward, and initiated a lawsuit against the Cooke estate some months later in the amount of $200,000, a case from which she did receive some damages after Cooke's widow sued her for Cooke's funeral expenses. The trial was surprisingly brief, and after interviews with both Franklin and Boyer, the defense's ability to cross-examine the primary witnesses was, according to firsthand accounts, "severely limited."[78] No mention was allowed of the two women's backgrounds, either Boyer's life as a prostitute or Franklin's former life as a Madame. Further, it was ruled to be

---

[74] Ed Gordon, NPR RADIO, Interview of Peter Guralnick, Nov. 6, 2005

[75] Daniel Wolff, "He Gave Us Water: You Send Me: the Life and Times of Sam Cooke", in The Threepenny Review, No. 67, Autumn 1996, p. 19

[76] Lydia Hutchinson, Performing Songwriter

[77] Lydia Hutchinson, Performing Songwriter

[78] David Wolff, The Threepenny Review

inadmissible evidence that Franklin had shot a man to death six months prior in an almost identical circumstance. Furthermore, neither the police nor the court took the time to review "contradictions between the night manager's testimony and the forensic and medical evidence,"[79] contradictions that have still not been explained.

In the end, the incident was deemed to be "justifiable homicide" by the court, and Cooke, despite his celebrity status, was dubbed "just another unidentified rapist killed in Watts."[80] In fact, Cooke's identity was not known until the following Monday after the shooting, and the family hired a private detective to investigate details of the case, but to no avail. Cooke's sister, Agnes Cooke-Hoskins, took up the brunt of the family defense of Cooke's reputation, declaring that "my brother was first class all the way. He would not check into a $3 motel."[81] And yet, without question, one writer noted that "there he was at a $3 a night motel with a prostitute at 3 am."[82] Cooke seemed to feel no need to conceal his identity, and the couple signed the motel register, as Franklin had requested, as Mr. and Mrs. Sam Cooke.

A month after the conclusion of the trial, Elisa Boyer was again arrested for prostitution, and some months later, she was charged with second degree murder in the death of her current boyfriend. Barbara Cooke, at the time of her husband's death, was having an affair with a local bartender, but that ended amid the trial and a series of services held in honor of her husband. A short time later, she married Cooke's protégé, Bobby Womack, who was not yet 21 and was required to obtain his parents' permission in order for the marriage to proceed. Family, friends, and colleagues expressed disgust as Womack was seen driving Cooke's Ferrari around town, wearing his clothes and watch, and in possession of other items belonging to Barbara's recently deceased husband.

Funeral services for Sam Cooke were held in two cities, Los Angeles and Chicago, and thousands of mourners were present at each. His body lay in state for a period of three days in Los Angeles, with the service held at Mt. Sinai Baptist Church. Ray Charles, Lou Rawls, Bobby Bland, and Arthur Lee Simkins all performed, and Charles' rendition of "Angels Keep Watching over Me" was particularly noteworthy. Gospel singer Bessie Griffin, however, was so grief-stricken that she was unable to maintain her composure and "had to be carried off."[83] Cooke's $4,000 casket was covered with plexiglass so that no one could touch the body.

In addition to the breakdown of Ms. Griffin, the hyperbole of other accounts reflects the high state of emotion throughout the gathering. Etta James, after viewing the body, reported that his injuries were beyond description, and that from the blows of the broom handle, "his head [was]

[79] David Wolff, The Threepenny Review
[80] IMDb, Sam Cooke Biography
[81] New World Encyclopedia, Sam Cooke – www.newworldencyclopedia.org/entry/Sam-Cooke
[82] Dirt City Chronicles, Death By Misadventure, Sam Cooke – www.dirtchronicles.blogspot.com/2012/07/death-by-misadventure-sam-cooke.html
[83] ABKO, Artists, Sam Cooke

nearly separated from his shoulders, his hands were broken, and his nose mangled."[84] However, photographic evidence does not support James' account, or other similarly dramatic memories of those present.

A second service was held in Chicago, and Cooke's body was flown there before returning for interment at Forest Lawn Memorial Cemetery. The Tabernacle Baptist Church, as it turned out, was an insufficient space in which to accommodate the number of mourners, only allowing for about a third of those in attendance. Cooke's Chicago service required 50 police officers, and mourners stood in zero degree weather for hours on end. Eulogies were offered by Reverend Lewis Rawls and E. Rodney Jones of WDNO Radio.

The memorials had scarcely ended when conspiracy theories gained momentum all over the pop music world. Among the chief suspicions was that the mafia had taken part in Cooke's death since he had recently signed with producer Allen Klein. This purportedly "infuriated a few executives associated with the mob,"[85] and that in terms of the collective studio brass throughout parts of the industry, Cooke was "a marked man for white record executives."[86] Others reported that in a brief period of time before the incident at the Hacienda, Cooke was approached by a number of "shadowy figures,"[87] allegedly requesting to be cut in on some of Cooke's increasingly lucrative businesses. Cooke, according to these reports, made the serious mistake of declining. One thread of suspicion went so far as to claim that Barbara herself arranged her husband's death, and that she hinted at the possibility that Vincent was not his biological son.

Through it all, the Cooke family generally succeeded in remaining low-key at the suggestion of Charles Cook, Sr. As the gossip continued through the aftermath of the family's loss, so did Cooke's career, almost as if nothing had happened. At the time of his death, his popularity had peaked, and the broader audience seemed willing to overlook the unseemly nature of his death. In 1965, Cooke's unequaled rendition of an older song, "Unchained Melody," was released, a tune that had gone through numerous covers from several genres. In keeping with the versions sung by other "pure" vocalists, such as Johnny Mathis and Michael Jackson, Cooke's performance is backed up by a rich, saturated orchestration that includes harp and orchestral bells. In that year, "At the Copa" was released as well, a collection of the more docile aspect of Cooke's performance personality.

More family trouble erupted, however, when Cooke's young niece held her wedding in Chicago. Sam's brother Charles had already confronted Bobby Womack, now married to Cooke's widow, at a local motel for a "personal talk,"[88] threatening Womack's life if he ever

[84] ABKO, Artists, Sam Cooke
[85] Dirt City Chronicles
[86] Dirt City Chronicles
[87] Panache Report, the Mysterious Death of Sam Cooke –
    www.panachereport.com/channels/Old_schools_update/theMysteriousDeathofSamCooke.htm
[88] Rare Soul.com, Bobby Womack Marries Sam Cooke's Widow; Gets Pistol-Whipped, 02/24/13

appeared in Chicago again. Womack and wife Barbara, intent upon attending the wedding, decided that they were not willing to live in fear of Cooke's family and phoned Charles beforehand, announcing that they would be present. Barbara brought a loaded pistol with her to Chicago, and attempted to fire at Charles, who was beating Womack so severely that his teeth began to protrude through his lips. She was unaware that Womack had unloaded the pistol before their arrival. In a further complication of family affairs, Womack had apparently started a relationship with Barbara and Cooke's oldest daughter, Linda, who rejected him for his own brother Cecil. With him, she had seven children and moved the family to Africa.

Given the shocking nature of his death in December 1964, it's no surprise that throughout 1965, Cooke's songs remained "a mainstay in the top forty,"[89] although in the case of more religious listeners, the manner of his death somewhat tarnished his image. Only two months later, "Shake" reached the 7th spot for singles, and it would go on to be covered by some of the most famous artists of the next generation, including Otis Redding and Rod Stewart. Motown Studios responded to Cooke's death with a typically slick, elite tribute entitled "Remember Sam Cooke," as presented by The Supremes, singing in what the studio referred to at the time as "high negro style."[90] Cooke's importance as a mentor to artists such as Aretha Franklin and Otis Redding increased as their careers blossomed, and he would be continually referenced by famous rappers throughout the following decades, including The Roots, Nas, and the late Tupac Shakur. Live shows like the 1963 Miami Harlem Square performance would in time become some of the most revered performance collections ever assembled, and they represented Cooke's most authentic and unfettered stage personality.

In 1966, Cooke's own record company released "A Change Is Gonna Come," and the song so feared by the cautious heads at RCA fulfilled expectations by becoming one of the anthems at the forefront of both the civil rights and the protest movements. Cooke's efforts, made in response to Dylan's "Blowin' in the Wind," became the most pointed and controversial example of his entire professional output, and it secured him a place as "one of the many martyrs of the civil rights movement."[91]

Perhaps inevitably, Cooke's posthumous output did not fare quite so well as the '70s got underway, and poor-quality releases began to emerge that could not convey the true quality of his work, "mostly budget-priced compilations."[92] Barbara, whether out of financial need or ignorance as to how much the inventory was worth, sold her former husband's publishing company for a paltry $103,000, even as the catalog still generated three to five million dollars per year.

---

[89] Rolling Stone, Sam Cooke

[90] Mark Anthony Neal, Black Voices

[91] Mark Anthony Neal, Black Voices, September 18, 2014, Remembering Sam Cooke and the Sounds of Young America, Huffington Post – www.huffingtonpost.com/mark-anthony-neal/remembering-sam-cooke-sound-b-2280523.htm

[92] Bruce Eder, MSN Entertainment

Meanwhile, Cooke had failed to leave behind a will, resulting in year after year of legal battles, with the catalog lawsuits extending for more than half a century. These conflicts caused a delay with almost everything, including printed music and a planned biopic. His oldest daughter, Linda, sued ABKO over copyright violations, further claiming that the company was "not up to major standards to reproduce a major artist."[93] ABKO, formerly named KAGS, was put under new leadership by the appointment of Allen Klein, who maintained control over 152 of Cooke's classic compositions.

A 12 track collection entitled "The Best of Sam Cooke" was released in 1982. In a successful collaboration, Cooke sang all of the lead vocals, beautifully backed by old friend Lou Rawls. In 1986, Cooke was inducted into the Rock & Roll Hall of Fame, and "A Change Is Gonna Come" continued to enjoy prominence by being played in the 1992 biopic "Malcolm X," as well as at the first inauguration of Barack Obama. In 1993, Cooke was given the Chairman's Award from the Apollo Theater Foundation posthumously, and six years later, he received 1999's first Pioneer Award, given by the Rhythm & Blues Foundation. In the same year, he received the NARAS Grammy Lifetime Achievement Award.

In Los Angeles County, the state of Mississippi, and the city of Chicago, proclamations created a Sam Cooke Day in 2001, and he was a Legend Grammy Winner for Best Long Form Music Video from the collections of his live appearances. In 2005, the Library of Congress added "A Change Is Gonna Come" to the national registry for works that have exerted an abiding influence on the social and artistic conditions of the country.

Following a prolonged, purposeful silence from Cooke's family at the behest of his father, a biography was at last released in 2006 by nephew Erik Greene, entitled "Our Uncle Sam." The effort was an exhaustive and thoughtful project by Greene, who felt compelled to "add his family's perspective to the singer's life story."[94] Greene was born over a year after Cooke's death and makes no claim to being a primary source, so he presented his book as one that synthesizes the family stories and general perspective from those who were present in Cooke's life. Much was made of the man Cooke was behind the public curtain, the power of the music, and the many inconsistencies surrounding his death. Since Allen Klein came into possession of all musical control, and no one in the family trees draws any royalties from Cooke's life work, these perspectives also come without any commercial conflict of interest.

Peter Guralnick, Sam Cooke's leading biographer, produced an award-winning documentary on the artist in 2007, entitled "The Sam Cooke Legend." That was followed by a second project announced four years later. Casting began in earnest during 2013, and all the necessary rights were given by Cooke's estate. For the next step, it was reported that "the script has been written,

[93] Brittany M. Walker, Carl Franklin to Direct New Cooke Biopic – Casting Has Begun, Euroweb – www.euroweb.com/2013/03/carl-franklin-to-direct-sam-cooke-in-biopic-casting-has-begun
[94] David Krajicek, Crime Library

and [that] Carl Franklin will direct."[95]

Chapter 5: Sam Cooke's Legacy

If people were to negate the work of an artist out of disapproval of his personal life, virtually all religious-oriented works would be invalid. In order to appreciate the legacy of whatever great works are left by performers, the authentic feeling behind that work may be probed, but all the best works in history were written by flawed individuals without exception, and they require a separate evaluation unless the music shares content with the personal transgression. Some merely viewed Cooke's passing as tragic, while others saw it as God's punishment for his crossing over from the sacred to the profane. However, no matter what Sam Cooke was like in life or death, it's almost impossible to overstate the influence he had on American music. From an overarching perspective, Cooke arguably mended a "falsely created gap between black and white music in the 50s,"[96] when most of the rural forms that coalesced into the largest markets shared great similarities. Rural artists who listened to all the music native to their own roots were crossing racial lines naturally without being conscious of it, but it was definitely different in the cities, where the characteristics of black and white music were more distinctly separated. Sam Cooke's career was unquestionably split into two phases, one being gospel and the other being secular, but in the '50s, it was nearly impossible for a black artist to live in both without disdain from one side or the other, particularly from the black gospel world. Cooke would take a daring risk by launching an entirely new career that resulted in such hits as "You Send Me."

In addition to being a pioneer in the new form and a great singer by any standards, Cooke was also one of the first black artists to bridge this forced separation and successfully straddle the world of religious and secular music, a taboo in black society. However, as a first-rate gospel singer in the early years of his career, Cooke was able to accomplish this by "put[ting] the spirit of the black church into popular music"[97] and creating an atmosphere of spiritualistic secularism, melded with his vocal beauty, that tenuously straddled the reverent and the romantic. And while he never truly settled on a specific individual style with his "warm, confessional voice"[98] since he was able to excel across genres, many consider him to be "the definitive soul singer" in the history of the art.

As the original link between the distinctly separate styles of gospel and soul, Cooke went on to create a "diverse repertoire"[99] equally embraced by white and black audiences, setting a standard for the next wave of artists by "merging gospel with secular themes."[100] As the style's first great performing artist, Cooke's vocal excellence captured the fascination of black and white

---

[95] Brittany M. Walker, Euroweb

[96] Encyclopedia.com, Sam Cooke – www.encycopedia.com/topic/Sam_Cooke.aspx

[97] American Masters, Sam Cooke, Crossing Over – www.pbs.org/

[98] Rock & Roll Hall of Fame, Sam Cooke Biography – www.rockhall.com/inductees/sam-cooke/bio/

[99] Rolling Stone, Sam Cooke – www.rollingstone.com/music/artists/sam-cooke/biography

[100] Rolling Stone, Sam Cooke

audiences as well, and history increasingly views him as "the very first superstar of soul,"[101] if not the genre's "founding father."[102] This bringing together of the races as an audience would alter almost everything about the music industry, including the ways radio, publishing, and recording studios worked.

By the time his switch to secular music was complete, Cooke had established his own record label and publishing company, had negotiated deals with major institutions of the industry that were previously impossible to get for any non-white artist, and won over an entirely new audience with his "crystal clear, velvet smooth voice set to up-tempo tunes,[103]" established ballads, and a series of brilliant originals, all of which came with a finely calculated "photogenic smile and business acumen."[104] For an African-American artist, these were firsts on every count, and in his brief, groundbreaking career, Cooke managed to have 29 hits reach the Top 20 in a period of roughly eight years.

To many, it is a mystery that Cooke's name is not the first one that immediately springs to mind whenever soul is mentioned. Perhaps his involvement in the earliest part of the form's progression opened the way for others but left him somewhat forgotten along the way because his career was cut short. One historian believes, however, that "he never sat still long enough to become as big a star as he might have deserved...[and that his] restlessness never allowed his talent to catch up with his ambition."[105] Nonetheless, it's somewhat ironic that given all the dysfunction that beset Sam Cooke and his circle of family, friends and professional acquaintances, there is a positive and constructive legacy to the form which he helped to create. Soul may have started as an expression of being African-American, but it has since become part of the national mainstream's pop music canon. No listener who approaches the soul music of Sam Cooke and the generation he mentored can be barred from the music's beauty by any issues of race, era, or culture, as it speaks to universal and deep human emotions. Furthermore, at the bottom of it all, soul wishes its listener well, regardless of any other social consideration. In the words of Robert Palmer of *The New York Times*, "There is something intrinsic to the nature of black popular music...without diluting its own essential blackness, it reaches out beyond itself – it wants everyone to feel all right."[106]

Sam Cooke may have struggled throughout his life to feel all right as a result of personal issues and social forces beyond his control, but as his music has always promised to those who are feeling down, change will come.

Otis Redding

[101] Jimmie Elliott, Mississippi Writers and Musicians – www.mswritersandmusicians.com/musicians/Sam-Cooke.html

[102] Bio.com, Sam Cooke Biography

[103] Bio.com, Sam Cooke Biography

[104] James Nadal, All About Jazz, Sam Cooke – www.musicians.allaboutjazz.com/samcooke

[105] Jacob Ganz, NPR Music

[106] Robert Palmer, "The Pop Life," New York Times, January 29, 1986

Chapter 1: Early Years

"As I was growing up, I did a lot of talent shows. I won fifteen Sunday nights straight in a series of talent shows in Macon. I showed up the sixteenth night, and they wouldn't let me go on any more. Whatever success I had was through the help of the good Lord." – Otis Redding

Otis Ray Redding, Jr. was born in Dawson, Georgia of Terrell County, on September 9th, 1941, three months before the Japanese invasion of Pearl Harbor, yet there are still differing opinions on his family background, particularly concerning his father. Some say that Redding came from a "sharecropping and farming family,"[107] while others list his parents' professions as those of a maintenance man and maid. Regardless, with Otis Sr.'s life's wish to become a Southern-style pastor, the atmosphere was not conducive to a love of secular music.

Eventually, his father was able to obtain a place as a lay preacher, despite not being fully ordained, at the Vineville Baptist Church in Macon, moving his family there when Otis Jr. was five years of age. The son of a Baptist minister himself, Otis Sr. took more than a dim view of Redding's musical interests, and in that regard he was backed up by the church, which characterized all non-sacred composition as "the devil's music."[108] Like so many black artists who would emerge in the industry throughout the '50s after growing up in the Southern black church and its choral traditions (including with fathers in the clergy), Redding spent a great deal of his childhood in the choir of Vineville Baptist and was steeped in the highly ecstatic, crisp energy of black gospel music. The family lived in a residence on the Robins Air Force Base for a time, where Otis Sr. worked during the week, but due to his poor health[109] and an incident in which the residence was heavily damaged by fire, they were forced to return to the Tindal Housing Project of Macon. The underlying cause of Otis Sr.'s ill health was eventually revealed to be tuberculosis, which would place an enormous financial burden on Redding's mother, Fannie.

Redding's teen years were almost entirely focused on providing supplemental support for his mother, but his insistence on becoming a singer, long before he was even aware of having an employable talent or voice, bordered on the maniacal, costing him several transitional jobs along the way. For a short time, he worked as a gas station attendant, and later as a well-digger, but in a stint as a parking attendant, he was fired for singing on the job. His employer could find him almost anytime sitting in the parked cars and crooning away, learning how to negotiate the subtleties of his voice. The same was true of his job at the local hospital, where he was eventually let go for "singing in the halls"[110] at full voice, no matter the hour of day or night.

Eventually, Redding found a niche by which he could provide steady money to the family.

---

[107] New World Encyclopedia, Otis Redding – www.newworldencyclopedia.org/entry/Otis-Redding

[108] New World Encyclopedia, Otis Redding

[109] NNDB, Tracking the Entire World, Otis Redding – www.nndb.com/people/000062679/

[110] Encyclopedia.com, Otis Redding

Dropping out of Ballard High School in the 10th grade, he entered the network of talent shows that were so prolific throughout the South, and for a brief period, brought home $25 each week from ongoing success at events, such as the one run by prominent local musician Gladys Williams. Each first prize was $5. On Saturday mornings, he sang at the Roxy Theater for a series of talent shows sponsored by DJ King Bee (Hamp Swain). The format of the weekly talent contest was called the "Teenage Party," broadcast on WIBB of Macon, a contest that Redding won 15 times in succession before being barred from further participation. Hamp "King Bee" Swain is credited as being one of the first to discover Redding's talent.

Appearing at a greater frequency through his teens, Redding reached a turning point in 1959, a time in which he was able to take his first professional steps with a band that could be described as cohesive and viable. It was also the year in which he would meet the woman who would become his wife two years later, Zelma Atwood, with whom he would have four children (Dexter, Karla, Otis III, and Demetria, adopted shortly after his death). Zelma recognized his passion for a career in music at once, and despite harboring serious doubts about the speculative nature of the venture, waited patiently while he worked as a group musician with a band known as the Upsetters, a former back-up band to Little Richard. In fact, Zelma rarely saw Otis during their first year together, but both of them grew confident as his opportunities increased and his success grew more tangible. Hiring Phil Walden, an old high school friend, as his manager, Redding was (to Zelma's surprise) able to manage a sustained income that year, despite having to spend so much of his time away.

Little Richard

Phil Walden

While Walden spent time overseas in the armed forces, his younger brother, Alan, took over the management of Redding's early career, and both brothers would go on to executive careers in music, with Phil founding the prominent label Capricorn Records and both brothers joining with Redding in a publishing venture. By the end of 1959, Redding had sung regularly at the Grand Duke Club of Macon, without a doubt a significant upgrade in terms of local venues.

Chapter 2: The Beginning of Redding's Career

In 1960, Redding made his first contacts with a band whose boundaries extended past the locale of Macon, Georgia. While appearing at the "Teenage Party," Redding was approached by an eccentric and "outrageous, left-handed guitarist"[111] named Johnny Jenkins, leader of a band dubbed the Pinetoppers. Not prone to shyness, Jenkins came forward to tell Redding that his back-up band "just wasn't making it"[112] and asked if he could fill in for a stretch of the following set. Redding had, by this time, played every week on WIBB for $6 per appearance and had enjoyed some success with Jazzbo Brown and the House Rockers, as well as a brief period of time with Macon's Willie and the Panthers. The local press had taken to calling him "Otis Rocking Robin Redding," but with his limited time spent on stage, Jenkins' observation was accurate; there were performance matters still to be worked out.

Johnny Jenkins

---

[111] New World Encyclopedia, Otis Redding
[112] Encyclopedia.com, Otis Redding

In the beginning, Redding seemed unable to sing and dance at the same time, so his stage strategy was to merely shake his torso while his feet remained planted. Such a limitation was no longer in evidence by the time he reached the legendary Monterey Festival of 1967 and other large public venues. Although his first recordings are said to have been made with the Pinetoppers at Stax, the first was actually "She's Alright," recorded with the Finer Arts label and released under the name of Otis and the Shooters. "Fat Gal" and "Shout Bamalama" followed soon after. Prior to his association with the Pinetoppers, Redding had been a member of Pat Teacake's band until Pinetoppers founder Johnny Jenkins left in the early '60s, with Redding following behind soon after.

Names were typically changeable for bands who did not want to appear on a label with a minor or new artist, and they were sometimes altered to avoid legal conflicts with other studio contracts. Among Redding's first recordings, some were made for Trans World, and later (as a Pinetopper) on the Confederate label, but Volt Records was an affiliate of Stax, founded by Jim Stewart and his sister, Estelle Axton, and eventually became Redding's best-known recording home. In this era, Stax and Motown were "the two most important record labels in America for bringing black music into the mainstream,"[113] and with Redding's rudimentary musical education and attachment to traditional roots, Stax was, by far, the more suitable choice.

---

[113] Rock & Roll Hall of Fame, Jim Stewart – www.rockhall.com/inductees/jim-stewart/

Victor Chapa's picture of the Stax Museum, a replica of the original recording studio in Memphis

Soul music represented the premier musical expression of the generalized black experience of America, particularly in the South and specific northern points like Chicago. As a genre, however, it was less specialized in the beginning before finding its way into a myriad of various forms, in which the great soul artists of the '50s and '60s thrived. At the heart of the intent, however, soul music took on the stylistic trappings of the Southern black church, and superimposed it onto a more public industry, "through the transmutation of gospel and rhythm & blues into a funky, secular testifying."[114] With undercurrents of regionalized styles, "based in black gospel, country, and 'earlier forms of rhythm and blues,'"[115] the Stax sound stood as the direct opposite to the smooth Motown musical personality, and recorded examples of rural Southern songs more in the manner by which they were originally expressed by county artists who shared more traditional musical roots. At Stax, Otis Redding and his contemporaries, while no less expressive than the Motown greats, were not required to fit such a narrow studio mold,

---

[114] Rock & Roll Hall of Fame, Otis Redding Biography – www.rockhall.com/inductees/otis-redding/bio/
[115] Rob Bowman, "The Stax Sound: A Musicological Analysis", in *Popular Music*, Vol. 14 No. 3, Oct., 1995

conform to such a formulaic musical behavior, or record such a restrictive band of finely-targeted songs for a specifically researched and pinpointed demographic.

The years of 1960 and 1961 represented the start of many important changes in Otis Redding's life. Marrying Zelma Atwood and expecting his first child were the most significant events on the personal front, and he also began to tour for the first time with a band capable of assembling a true touring itinerary, not to mention connecting with a bona fide record company. Despite Johnny Jenkins' strong instincts for Redding's artistic bent, the initial opening to work with the Pinetoppers was a narrow one with scant opportunities for singing. The Pinetoppers were "favorites on the Southern college circuit,"[116] and they were eventually invited to audition, then record, for Stax Records in Memphis. The sole reason for Otis Redding being taken along was that Johnny Jenkins had no license to drive; Redding's presence on that career-changing trip was, therefore, mostly as a driver and roadie.

During the ensuing Memphis session, a short 40 minute stretch of studio time remained at the end of the allotted time, so Redding asked if he could take up a few minutes to record one or two songs. Jim Stewart, president and co-owner of the company, allowed it, although band members were said to have objected, in part because the session was intended to serve as a Pinetopper audition, not an hour for the band driver's wish to play around in the studio. Furthermore, some of the musicians within the studio's home band, Booker T. and the M.G.'s, mistook Redding as a roadie as they watched him unload and tote equipment.

[116] Chris Starrs, New Georgia Encyclopedia, Arts & Culture, Otis Redding (1941-1967), 2005 – www.georgiaencyclopedia.org/articles/arts-culture/otis-redding-1941-1967

Booker T. and the M.G.'s

When Redding approached Al Jackson (the house drummer for Stax) and asked him to play a few chords on the piano to help him out, Redding didn't even know the key that would best suit his vocal range or the name of the rhythmic figure he wanted for the improvised accompaniment. As Jackson recalled, Redding sang the figure out and simply asked him "if you can just get me some of those da-da-das"[117] – triplets, as he was soon to learn, the same figure that underpins the waltz. Jackson chose the key of B flat Major, which turned out to be a good decision, and Redding would maintain a preference for it through the rest of his career.

Nonetheless, what resulted from those few improvised minutes was the luscious and

---

[117] NPR Music, Music Articles

memorable "These Arms of Mine," a song that beautifully demonstrated Redding's lyrical side and his "dolce" (sweet) vocal characteristics, one of his sympathetic connections to Sam Cooke. Jackson, who immediately sought out Stewart, told him, "You got to come and hear this guy's voice, you know?"[118] He also remembered, "We all fell on the floor, of course, and that song on one note…"[119] Stewart was persuaded to come back and hear Redding personally, despite the grumbling of band members, some of whom were already on their way to night gigs and had to unpack their instruments from the car. Redding, however, was signed immediately, and thus his career progressed despite his naiveté about how anything in the industry worked and the fact he possessed no formal knowledge of musical structure or function.

Chapter 3: Stax

Since Redding was completely untrained as to the workings of a studio or live stage on the upper levels, there was a lot of work to do. Just as he had referred to triplets as "da-da-das," that condition would grow exponentially larger as he encountered larger challenges, but colleagues, now won over, were tremendously helpful in getting him untracked. Indeed, as one writer put it, Redding had "so many ideas…so much music in him…traffic jams basically what it was…and he needed help getting them worked out."[120] Booker T. Jones, when asked to compare the young Redding with Presley and Sinatra as part of a commentary on his album "Sound the Alarm," noted that Redding was "striking…but [at the same time] a very unassuming person." Jones' following remarks seemed to suggest that Redding was inordinately preoccupied with time already spent and lost on trying to get his career started, perhaps a reaction to beginning from farther behind, and that he was desperate to push the process and move things forward. Jones explained, "Redding seemed to be possessed all the time. Nobody was quite sure what was going with him. He just seemed to be in a hurry. Not a hurry – obsessed."[121]

"These Arms of Mine," the song that started it all for Otis Redding, subsequently became a "moderate cross-over hit for the Stax affiliate, Volt Records."[122] The song was successful enough to warrant the release of several more singles, including "I've Been Loving You Too Long," "Respect," "Try a Little Tenderness," and "Chained and Bound," employing the studio's house band, Booker T. and the M.G.'s, as a regular back-up ensemble. Redding had begun his Stax career more as a guitarist than vocalist, but his extraordinarily high energy in the studio, and his vocal abilities, opened opportunities at every turn. In the following years, the six albums and the 30 singles he released through Stax would be further magnified by his gift for live performing. He became an eventual favorite at the Apollo Theater in Harlem, the Howard in Washington, D.C., the Whisky A Go Go in Los Angeles, and in cities and choice venues throughout Europe thanks to his two tours of that continent.

---

[118] NPR Music, Music Articles
[119] NPR Music, Music Articles
[120] NPR Music, Music Articles
[121] The Guardian, Booker T. Jones – www.theguardian.com/music/2013/sep/12/booker-t-jones-sound-alarm-interview
[122] NNDB, Otis Redding

Meanwhile, Johnny Jenkins, the man who got Redding his real start, faded from the music scene in a stroke of bitter irony. Possessing all the guitar chops and promotional charm imaginable, Jenkins, "the pre-Hendrix guitar wizard who was there at the beginning with Otis Redding...wouldn't travel when the ride star beckoned, and retreated into the shadows of 'bitterness and paranoia.'"[123] In Jenkins' defense, his career, previously managed by Phil Walden, was put on hold and ground to a virtual halt while Walden turned his attentions to developing Redding. Jenkins must have felt a special sting at such neglect after having provided Redding with his first opportunity to make good in the industry.

Stax Records did not establish its best years or develop the fame of its best artists by being insular and disconnected from the concert-going public. In fact, much of their clout in the mid-to-late '60s came from first tier groups such as Sam & Dave, who began touring under Stax's leadership in 1966 and topped the studio's sales charts at the time. However, according to author Peter Guralnick, the appearance of Otis Redding altered the racial audience demographic of Stax to such a degree that record and ticket sales from a new white audience brought them to a higher level. In *Sweet Soul Music*, Guralnick asserts that Redding's presence "made Stax a byword in soul circles...opened the world of Southern Soul to large-scale white audiences,"[124] and helped to usher in an era in which collaborative efforts required "blacks and whites [to] work as a team."[125]

[123] Peter Guralnick, "Sweet Soul Music: Rhythm and Blues and the Southern Dream of Freedom", Review by Robert Cochran in *The Journal of American Folklore,* Vol. 100 No. 396, April-June, 1987, p.224

[124] Encyclopedia.com, Otis Redding

[125] Peter Guralnick, Journal of American Folklore

Sam & Dave

The style of working so prevalent at Stax reflected a different sort of creativity from Motown in that it pandered to all of the brilliant and spontaneous impulses that might occur to even the least among the band members. Highly improvisatory, the artists at the studio referred to the emergence of their best creations as "spontaneous arrangements."[126] The studio allowed artists to flirt with instrumental elaborations, such as added strings or horn sections, but at the core, Stax allowed the music to remain in a far more raw state than did Motown. Strings, for example, were added to "I Love You More Than Words Can Say," but only "sporadically on the bulk of

---

[126] Encyclopedia.com, Otis Redding

Memphis-based recordings."[127] When used at all, the arrangements prevented the string section from taking any focus away from the singer.

Likewise, background vocals were used sparingly, partly perhaps out of budgetary concerns, but also because of the richness and "saturation" they brought to the background of each song's personality. The one area in which this rule went by the wayside was in almost anything recorded by Carla Thomas, who would record Redding's final album with him, "King and Queen," and with whom Stax had hoped to emulate Motown's magical combination of Marvin Gaye and Tammi Terrell. Thomas, however, was already well-established in R&B, and her audience was accustomed to the elaborate background filigree of her famous tracks.

[127] Rob Bowman, "The Stax Sound: A Musicological Analysis", in *Popular Music*, Vol. 14 No. 3, Oct., 1995

Carla Thomas

Otherwise, Stewart liked to keep things "raw [and] funky."[128] Orchestral backup was all but unheard of at Stax, and if a string player was to be hired, it would amount to no more than one - an occasional violin, viola, or cello, but no massive sections borrowed from the well of regional orchestral talent, as in the case of Motown.

That said, Redding was a leading figure in the insertion of horn sections, considered by the management to be the equivalent of a vocal backup group. Horns were somewhat less obtrusive than string sections or voices, in Stewart's opinion, and a good deal less expensive. In rehearsal, Redding had an ongoing habit of humming or whistling any instrumental parts that were not yet written in or entirely formulated so that his colleagues would get the full picture of his vision, and more often than not, these added lines were meant for the horns. According to one musician at Stax, "He hummed a lot of horn lines to us – we took it from there, and they turned out to be Memphis Horn lines – Otis was a good teacher. He taught us a lot about rhythm, [and] he loved the horns."[129] This was obviously high praise for an artist who could not even identify a simple triplet at the beginning of his time with Stax. By the time Redding, his filled in parts, and Booker T.'s imaginative house band were finished, the typical Stax song foundation was built on its signature qualities, "sultry organ work, a lithe rhythm section and lots of meaty horn accents,"[130] a background much less likely to intrude on the singer and much less likely to emit impressions of over-arranged "show business" characteristics that would pull the music too far from its origins.

Of the three general moods into which Redding's voice fit so perfectly, including the high energy "ecstasy" song and the sweet, lyric ballad, he was also blessed with an excellent sense of humor, which he often used in the occasional jaunty, satirical song. This fit in perfectly with a specific pet peeve of Jim Stewart: an edict against the use of minor chords that darkened the personality of the musical setting. Thus, despite the minor mode's significant role in the structure of all great forms, for Stax, "minor chords were avoided due to the aesthetic whims of owner/producer." The resulting harmonic brightness, however, was amenable to satire and cheerful texts, and they were particularly effective in some of the early tongue-in-cheek songs such as "Fat Gal." In many of Redding's best examples, he either attempted to evoke a passionate sexuality toward himself as the singer/narrator, or on the less serious side, he was likely to declare open season on female anatomy and movement. For example, the whimsical "Fat Gal" opens with the verse, "She's standing in the way, and that ain't all, she's not very big, she's not very small. But every time she move she has to wiggle when she walk."[131] And on "Shout Bamalama," Redding made one of his first "foray[s] into Little Richard shouting."[132]

[128] Rob Bowman, Popular Music, p. 307
[129] Rob Bowman, Popular Music, p.307
[130] Randy Lewis, L.A. Times, Booker T. Resurrects Memphis Sound With 'Sound the Alarm." – June 25, 2013
[131] Agony Shorthand, Pinetoppers, "Shout Bamalama/Fat Gal" – www.agonyshorthand.com/pinetoppers-shout-bamalama-fat-gal-45.html
[132] Agony Shorthand, Pinetoppers

Another directive from Stewart may sound to some like pointless eccentricity, but it actually turned out to be an important component of selling records to female buyers who comprised the majority in the market of that era. Stewart wanted less emphasis on the high-range instruments and an "un-Motownish" use of deeper tonal colors. Redding colleague Steve Cropper put it succinctly, "We didn't like the high end. Women bought more records than men, and they were offended by the high end."[133]

The bulk of original songs coming out of the Stax Studio and Volt Records were created by one of a few songwriting teams that included the best of the in-studio talents, including teams like Isaac Hayes and David Porter, William Bell and Booker T. Jones, Eddie Floyd and Steve Cropper, and Otis Redding, either writing alone or in collaboration with Cropper. In addition, Rufus and Carla Thomas were both excellent songwriters. The bulk of Stax's recording activity was centered in Memphis, and with the concentrated personnel of fewer artists than the giant Motown, the Stax identity remained distinctive and more easily replicated throughout the 1960s.

---

[133] Rob Bowman, Popular Music, p. 307

Roland Godefroy's picture of Cropper

Isaac Hayes

By 1963, the release of the song that had started it all, "These Arms of Mine," brought it to #20 on the R&B charts, and 9 months after the final recording session for that song, Redding was invited to perform it at the Apollo Theater for a taped live concert, where he also demonstrated his best stage moves on "Shake" and "Satisfaction." These were phenomenal career years for Redding, and bassist Don "Duck" Dunn recalled in a later interview that "Otis would come in, and he'd just bring everybody up. You wanted to play with Otis. He brought out the best in you."[134]

1963 and 1964 brought more successes, with singles like "Pain in My Heart," "That's What My Heart Needs," "Mr. Pitiful," and "That's How Strong My Love Is." "Mr. Pitiful," another satirical example, was based on a remark made by a famous DJ suggesting that Redding looked and sounded "pitiful" when he was singing ballads. The studio's musical response, co-written with Steve Cropper, was not only a commercial success but served as the first of Redding's pieces to receive significant air time from a larger number of radio stations in the north.

By 1965, Redding had become a proven businessman and entrepreneur, and far more savvy

---

[134] Rock & Roll Hall of Fame, Otis Redding Biography

with his money than many fellow stars. In the year that he moved his family to the "Big O Ranch," 25 miles north of Macon and naturally named after the Big "O" himself, Redding also put together his own record and publishing companies, Jotis Records and Redwal Music, exponentially increasing his financial success. The name for Jotis Records was a derivative of Redding and Joe Galkin, a fellow producer and musician who had worked at Atlantic and Stax. Jotis would produce for Arthur Conley when Stax showed too little enthusiasm for his collaborative work with Redding. Redwal Music, the publishing company, was founded by Redding, manager Phil Walden and his brother, Alan, in 1965, and immediately set to compiling a dynamic and lucrative catalog.

Despite his hard work in the music industry, Redding's pride and joy was the ranch. Zelma would continue to live at the ranch permanently after Redding's death, and she recalled in interviews how much he loved the place and wished that he could spend more time there. As Redding himself once put it, "If I were to leave the U.S., I'd live in England. But I'd never leave the U.S. I own a 400-acre farm in Macon, Georgia. I raise cattle and hogs. I own horses, too. I love horses as much as singing. I like to hunt on horseback."

In addition to the ranch, Redding owned a private plane, as was fashionable among '60s stars, and once leaving the menial work and local touring of the early years, business ran smoothly for him. Able to detour many of the problems experienced by other artists and their financial partners, he "got paid, without the usual horror stories of being ripped off by promoters, agents, managers, or record company executives."[135] Furthermore, rather than letting the business of Redwal Publishing run itself or entrusting it to others, Redding monitored Jotis and Redwal carefully, remaining "very active in the company's operation."[136] The personal conviction that "music could be a universal force, bringing together different races and cultures, was central to Otis' philosophy,"[137] and likewise, it did no harm in business terms either. Redding took the same philosophy with him on the road, and the inspired response among his diverse audiences seemed indistinguishable from one race to another, whether at the Apollo or among the increasingly white audiences of London or Paris.

1965 also brought a major release for Redding that both defined the prestige of his career and captured the spirit of Southern soul perfectly, placing him in the midst of the greatest artists ever to sing it. As with other historical examples, such as leading albums of The Beatles, this abiding symbol of Redding's best work was recorded in an absurdly brief amount of studio time, spanning roughly 24 hours. The album, "Otis Blue: Otis Redding Sings Soul," has since been hailed as "a virtual Soul music primer"[138] for anyone approaching the genre of soul for the first time. That was important, for many in the era of the mid-'60s, particularly white audiences, were

[135] Otis Redding, the King of Soul – www.otisredding.com/#&panel1-9
[136] Otis Redding. Bio 7 – www.otisredding.com/anything_slides/bio-7/
[137] Otis Redding. Bio 7
[138] Rock & Roll Hall of Fame, Otis Redding Biography

doing just that.

Redding's success snowballed with the increased output of his albums and numerous singles, as well as through his own performances. One of the most famous songs on the album was "Respect," the song most famously performed by Aretha Franklin. With an altered text to fit the gender, Franklin's sisters, Erma and Carolyn, provided an individualistic background that Redding would never have imagined, including making liberal use of a favorite catch-phrase of the era, "sock it to me," which now sounds anachronistic and almost comedic.

As it turned out, the timing of Redding's 1965 album was excellent, albeit for unfortunate reasons; Sam Cooke, among the most brilliant vocalists in soul music, was shockingly shot to death in December 1964, and three of his songs were featured on the Redding album. The album also featured the single "I've Been Loving You Too Long," co-written with Jerry Butler. It was Redding's first song to reach the Top 40. The album also included a cover of Sam Cooke's "Shake," which would later cause such a sensation at the Monterey Festival, as well as "A Change is Gonna Come," Cooke's social sensation and anthem-to-be for the civil rights movement. An archetypal rendition of The Rolling Stones' hit "Satisfaction" rounded out the album. One of Redding's singles, "I Can't Turn You Loose/Just One More Day," also achieved great success in 1965, and his cover of The Temptations' hit "My Girl" was a sensation in the United Kingdom as well.

Sam Cooke

Redding followed that album up with "The Soul Album" in 1966, which also consisted of covers and originals, but that was not as acclaimed as Redding's subsequent studio album, "Complete & Unbelievable: The Otis Redding Dictionary of Soul," released later that same year. For this album, which would end up being the final album released before his death in 1967, the cover displayed a picture of a tall, smiling Redding in academic cap and gown, ready to teach the listener everything about the genre, and along the bottom of the jacket, in large block letters, was spelled the racially stereotypical phrase "My My My." In a mixture of high-profile covers and a handful of Redding originals, two singles stood out: "Fa-Fa-Fa-Fa-Fa (Sad Song)" and "Try a Little Tenderness." Successful covers included "You're Still My Baby" by Chuck Willis, "Lord Have Mercy" by Isaac Hayes and David Porter, the old and revered "Sweet Lorene," co-written by Hayes and Alvertis Isbell, and "Day Tripper" by The Beatles. Rounding out the originals were the less well-known "My Lover's Prayer," "She Put the Hurt on Me," "Ton of Joy," and "Hawg for You." Following such a string of successes in the studio, the National Academy of Recording Arts & Sciences nominated Redding for three award categories in1967.

Promotional image of Redding for the single "Fa-Fa-Fa-Fa-Fa (Sad Song)"

Chapter 4: 1967

The final year of Otis Redding's life was made all the more ironic and tragic by the nature of his continuous artistic breakthroughs, including his most iconic song. Enjoying ongoing success with his tours of Europe, where he played somewhat less well with Parisians who had developed a fondness for Sam & Dave, his star rose ever higher in Britain, and all appearances pointed to a career that was gathering speed despite its already prodigious success. That year, Redding was named the number one vocalist among British audiences in *Melody Maker Magazine*.

Returning home to Macon, Redding began working with fellow soul singer Arthur Conley, and together the two co-wrote "Sweet Soul Music." Redding and Conley had intended to form a professional alliance as both writers and performers, but such a pairing was discouraged by Stax, so the two worked away from Memphis during their brief but fruitful collaboration. "Sweet Soul Music" made its way to #2 on the R&B charts.

Arthur Conley

Meanwhile, Redding and Carla Thomas returned to the top 30 in both the U.S. and Britain with the satirical duet "Tramp." In the playful hit single, Redding poses as Thomas' mate, and she "dismiss[es] him for looking…"[139] Still reigning as the "Queen of Memphis Soul,"[140] and a major artist for Stax, the collaboration on both the single and the ensuing album, "Tell It Like It

---

[139] Encyclopedia.com, Otis Redding
[140] English! Info, Carla Thomas – www.english.turkcebilgi.com/Carla+Thomas

Is," could not help but be mutually beneficial to both artists' careers, precisely as Stax had hoped.

Despite a lengthy string of high-profile performances and collaborations in 1967, Redding was forced to take three months of vocal rest following surgery to eliminate polyps in his throat, a difficult assignment for one so driven to produce on a daily basis. Such a condition frequently occurs when a singer specializes in the type of "vocal burn" sound that artists such as Redding use for upbeat, sultry texts and various jazz effects. Fortunately, the condition was caught early and handled well, so at the end of the three months, Redding was back on a normal full-time schedule with no lingering effects.

Redding participated in the Stax touring review, "Hit the Road," before appearing as the only soul act in the 1967 Monterey Festival, where he was accepted whole-heartedly by audiences consisting of blacks, hippies, and middle-class whites. The Monterey Festival had been established by music executive Lou Adler and John Phillips of The Mamas & the Papas, and it was the premier event for rock, folk and blues musicians in its day, surpassed only by Woodstock two years later.

In retrospect, Redding would become "to soul singing what Hendrix was to the guitar,"[141] but Redding made no special effort to fit in with the hippie-oriented musical and fashion statements that seemed to dominate the festival, choosing rather to appear in his customary "dark green silk and mohair suits."[142] Playing his sets after dark and in the rain, he can be seen on video challenging the audience to accept him by throwing out the lead line "This is the love crowd, right?" The diverse Monterey audience didn't hesitate, cheering him without reservation. Redding also performed a set with Hendrix that has been described by critics as "explosive."[143] Despite the fact that Hendrix had an entirely different audience and was a favorite of the counterculture, while Redding represented more traditional black roots, the shared set stood out in a way few others could, and one reviewer claimed that together, "they set the stage on fire."[144] Likewise, Hendrix had not yet reached the full flower of his popularity, but when Redding entered the stage and got under way, it was the "only time at Monterey when 50,000 souls got up *en masse* and danced."[145] The two artists, from two disparate genres, gelled in a rare way, and "white audiences, better known as the 'love crowd,' were digging Otis Redding,"[146] despite his emergence as a newcomer to the hippie festival scene and to the revolutionary culture, green silk suit and all.

---

[141] John Ballon, Must Hear.com

[142] Oldies.com, Otis Redding Biography – www.oldies.com/artist-biography/Otis-Redding.html

[143] Oldies.com, Otis Redding Biography

[144] John Ballon, Must Hear.com

[145] John Ballon, Must Hear.com

[146] Otis Redding, the King of Soul

A. Vente's picture of Jimi Hendrix in 1967

Further appearances in prestigious venues, including engagements at New York Philharmonic Hall, Washington's Constitution Hall, and on *The Ed Sullivan Show* and *The Smothers Brothers Show*, provided the perfect preparation for a breakthrough hit that would elevate Redding's career status to that of a legendary artist. In late 1967, Redding recorded a song that sharply broke in style from any of the moods he had typically characterized in former compositions. In the Bay Area for engagements at the Filmore, Redding worked incessantly in the off-hours on a song that was not about the individual romantic and sexualized love story, or an immediate call to his audience for a collective sexual response; instead, the song encompassed the entire question of life, and most emphatically the quality of Redding's life, which he had at one point summed up as being entirely – and surprisingly - "about bad luck."[147] This in itself was not uncommon for the basis of a song, and the futility of living is a theme to which millions of listeners are perennially attracted, although one might not have thought that such was Redding's true autobiographical view.

"(Sittin' On) The Dock of the Bay" was written, at least in the later stages, in an idyllic setting aboard a rented house-boat in Sausalito, where Redding admitted that he was in a more relaxed

---

[147] NPR Music, Music Articles

and peaceful state than he had ever experienced. Road manager Speedo Sims remembered that during the time aboard the houseboat, Redding played The Beatles' new album, "Sgt. Pepper's Lonely Hearts Club Band," around the clock, much to Sims' distraction, but Redding was apparently drawing a tremendous sense of inspiration from it. Sims was confounded by the new song, such as it was at the time, and observed that "it was three or four days before I could gain any concept of where he was going…lyrically, it sounded weird. He was changing with the times. And I was looking at the times change."[148]

In fact, work on the song had lingered through the entire European tour, but had remained unfinished, except for a single verse scribbled on napkins and scratch paper, so un-formulaic was the idea in terms of Redding's usual songwriting fare. Cropper, who worked on the song with Redding, recalled, "Otis was one of those kind of guys who had 100 ideas. Anytime he came in to record, he always had 10 or 15 different intros or titles, or whatever. He had been at San Francisco playing The Fillmore, and he was staying at a boathouse, which is where he got the idea of the ship coming in. That's about all he had: 'I watch the ships come in and I watch them roll away again.' I took that and finished the lyrics. If you listen to the songs I wrote with Otis, most of the lyrics are about him. He didn't usually write about himself, but I did. 'Mr. Pitiful,' 'Fa-Fa-Fa-Fa-Fa (Sad Song)'; they were about Otis' life. 'Dock Of The Bay' was exactly that: 'I left my home in Georgia, headed for the Frisco Bay' was all about him going out to San Francisco to perform."

Of the recollections from this period, Sims' account is the only one that suggests turmoil in Redding's life, aside from the everyday mundane, at least according to the infamous Scott Freeman biography of Redding. It is claimed that Redding had "outgrown his marriage and fallen in love with Carla Thomas…[and] was feeling constrained by Stax Records."[149] These claims would so offend Redding's widow that she was prompted to take whatever action she could to prevent its success. Freeman also claimed that Redding was using this brief period of serenity to listen to Bob Dylan and The Beatles and even smoke pot, another uncharacteristic habit for the customarily clear-minded and well-directed artist and businessman. In a more familiar description of Redding's impatience to move forward, it is noted that he wanted his own label, one of a significant enough stature to produce records at a high level; even after having been given a great deal more leeway than almost all of the great Motown artists, it was Redding's intent to become a self-managing producer and control the product from the top down.

In November 1967, "(Sittin On') The Dock of the Bay" was recorded, and even in that seemingly final version, it was perceived as unfinished. Redding, now the co-writer, guitarist and producer, could not remember the words he had penned for the finale, so whistling covered the song's last bars before the fade-out section of the song, a custom entirely in keeping with

[148] Bill de Main, Performing Songwriter, "Otis Redding's '(Sittin' On) The Dock Of The Bay'" – www.performingsongwriter.com/otis-redding-sittin-dock-bay

[149] Bill De Main, Performing Songwriter

Redding's career when an instrumental part was missing. As fate would have it, those words were to remain incomplete, and the whistling remains perhaps the signature aspect of the song itself.

Chapter 5: Redding's Death and the Aftermath

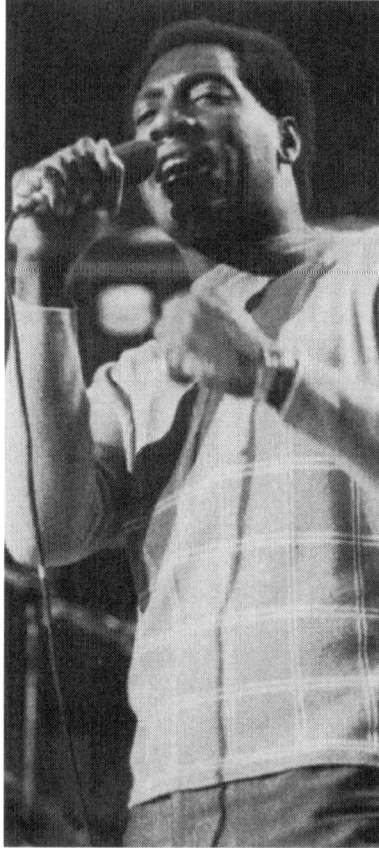

A promotional image of Redding for the single "When Something Is Wrong With My Baby"

On the 9th of December, 1967, Redding and the band appeared in Cleveland on a local TV show and performed sets for Leo's Casino. Like many other touring artists, Redding used his own private plane to make traveling easier; with appearance locations so regionalized, finding commercial flights that fit the itinerary was often problematic.

After the performances in Cleveland, Redding was due to perform at the Factory nightclub in Madison, Wisconsin the following day. Thus, even though weather and visibility were poor, Redding's plane took off and tried to land in fog on the afternoon of December 10. The pilot communicated with a small airfield in Madison shortly before the plane crashed into Lake Monona around 3:30 p.m., and only passenger, Ben Cauley of the Bar-Kays, survived the crash. Cauley had been sleeping, but he was jolted awake as he heard his bandmate Phalon Jones saying, "Oh no!" As a result, Cauley instinctively unbuckled his seat belt right around the time one wing of the plane hit the surface of the water and tore the fuselage open, ejecting Cauley into the freezing lake. Clinging to a cushion and unable to swim, Cauley "watched the rest of the passengers drown,"[150] unable to reach them. On the descent, Cauley remembered that Redding sat straight ahead of him, erect and silent, and he described Redding as "a groovy cat, like an older brother."[151]

Although Cauley could vividly remember listening to the other passengers screaming for help, the water was so cold that nobody could have survived longer than 15 minutes in it without dying from hypothermia. Cauley was rescued less than an hour after the crash because a few residents had seen the plane and heard the crash, but given the conditions, search and rescue teams could only spend 15 minutes at a time in the water due to the frigid temperatures. When scuba divers scoured Monona Lake, Redding was found still strapped into his seat, wearing a suit and tie, and video exists of recovery personnel removing him from the plane.

Redding's body was brought back to his home, and an understandably large group of mourners at his Macon funeral in the city auditorium included luminaries such as James Brown, Solomon Burke, and Wilson Pickett. His obituary was provided by his family, and wife Zelma described him as a "loving father, extraordinary friend, and legendary entertainer."[152] Redding was buried on the family estate.

Personal and professional tributes abounded from those closest to him. Booker T. Jones, who played the organ at his service, said later in *Rhythm & Blues* that "there was something pure about his personality, calm, dignified, vibrant. Stardom never changed him. He had a strong inner life. He was emotionally centered."[153] Members of his various bands spoke of those qualities as translating perfectly into a musical directness that made him and his art so distinct. Steve Cropper observed that Redding "worked in simple black…the man would make Gershwin sound greasy,"[154] and critic John Landau went so far as to claim that "Otis Redding *is* rock and roll."[155]

---

[150] Brian D'Ambrosio, Portal Wisconsin.org, "The Day Otis Redding Died, December 10, 1967, Lake Monona, Wisconsin"

[151] Brian D'Ambrosio, Portal Wisconsin.org

[152] The Telegraph, Otis Redding Obituary – www.legacy.com/obituaries/macon/obituary.aspx?pid=161540

[153] Encyclopedia.com, Otis Redding

[154] Encyclopedia.com, Otis Redding

It's still unclear why the plane crashed, but the crash that took Otis Redding's life occurred when the singer was still just 26 years old and stood on the cusp of seeing all of his professional dreams fulfilled. Many successful careers have barely begun by then, and Redding's death came mere days after recording his biggest hit. Despite Redding's shocking death, and the fact that it was obviously a difficult time for his colleagues, the studio demanded that something be completed that could be released immediately. That song was to be "(Sittin' On) The Dock of the Bay," and Cropper was preparing the final touches before Redding's body had even been found. Cropper, nicknamed "the Colonel," had been a master guitarist with the house band, Booker T. and the M.G.'s and had co-written extensively with Redding, so he understood more about the star's habits and tendencies as a writer. In that sense, it was only fitting that Cropper was the one to put the finishing touches on the song, and he would go on to be named the 39th greatest guitarist of all time by *Rolling Stone* and the 2nd best ever by *Mojo*.

As instructed, Redding's old writing partner went right to work, but he left the finale alone, including the whistled section of the fade-out. Cropper went to the effects library and inserted gull and wave sounds at the beginning, but for the most part, he did his best to avoid a major upheaval of Redding's initial vision. Cropper remembered that the two of them, once the European tour was over, had finished the song in a mere half hour. It was based on simple but effective harmonies, and the session with Cropper seemed to work with an almost magical ease: "Most songs only [have] two or three chord changes…the dynamics, the energy, the way we attacked it – that's hard to teach."[156] Of course, Redding was never able to hear the changes or the final product that was released by the studio soon after Cropper's efforts were completed.

All the while, Jim Stewart could not understand why Redding had thought it necessary to create a song that veered so far away from the traditional success that he had set through earlier releases. It was new to his ears, and out of context, and when all was said and done, he didn't really like the song, despairing that "it had no R&B in it whatsoever."[157] Donald Dunn agreed, admitting that for him to like a song, it had to fit into a narrow range of parameters: "If you couldn't dance to it, or it didn't make you want to hug a girl (i.e. slow dance), it wasn't worth shit."[158] Redding, however, was not dissuaded by either colleagues or any higher authority of the studio, guided by a deep inner conviction that, as he put it, "This is my number one record."[159]

As it turned out, Redding could not have been more correct. "(Sittin' On) The Dock of the Bay" would go on to be covered by everyone from Peggy Lee to Pearl Jam, becoming the sixth most performed song of the 20th century and receiving over 6 million radio performances in the ensuing years. In 1968, it became Redding's sole number one hit and sell over a million copies. In the process, Redding became the first musician to have a #1 hit posthumously.

---

[155] Free Webs.com, Soul in All Areas, Otis Redding – www.freewebs.com/soulinthehind/otisredding.htm

[156] Bill De Main, Performing Songwriter

[157] Bill De Main, Performing Songwriter

[158] Rob Bowman, Popular Music

[159] Bill De Main, Performing Songwriter

In a hurry to release everything possible while the topic of Redding's death was in the news and fresh in the public's mind, the studio was able to produce singles such as "The Happy Song (Dum Dum)," "Amen," "Papa's Got a Brand New Bag," and "Love Man" posthumously, even while "(Sittin' On) The Dock of the Bay" continued its unfaltering sales, mystifying Stewart the whole time. Warner Brothers released an album in 1970 taken from the Monterey Festival performance three years prior, and in the taped excerpts, as it had with the live audience, the Hendrix/Redding set still stood out.

By 1973, a compilation album entitled "16 Original Hits" had been released, and in addition to audio recordings, every scrap of film that could be found was arranged into one format or another and released. These include Redding's appearances in the Popcorn Festival (released in 1969), the Monterey Pop Festival, "Otis Redding: Remembering Otis," "Casey Kasem's Rock n Roll Goldmine: The Soul Years," "American Soul vol. 1," and "Dreams to Remember; The Legacy of Otis Redding." Several television appearances have also been re-released, including "Otis Redding/the Music Machine," The "Otis Redding Special," "Otis Redding, the Shadows of Knight," and "Buffalo Springfield/Otis Redding."

Well into the late '70s, Otis Redding's legacy could be seen reflected in the success of his children. Sons Dexter and Otis III formed the Reddings and recorded for the Believe in Dreams label, distributed by Columbia. The two became "active music producers and songwriters,"[160] while daughter Karla enjoyed an equal degree of success as an entrepreneur, including serving as Project Director for the Otis Redding Foundation. As the executor of the Otis Redding estate, Zelma, who served as the Reddings' manager for many years, never married again. She has, since her husband's death, managed all requests, including matters of sampling, the use of the artist's name and image, and the Otis Redding Memorial and Scholarship Fund.

In 1980, the Reddings scored their first top ten R&B hit with "Remote Control," recorded for Polydor Records, and in 1981, they watched as their father was honored with induction into the Georgia Music Hall of Fame. By 1987, Atlantic Records had released "The Otis Redding Story, Vol. 2," which featured hits that included "(Sittin' On) The Dock of the Bay."

In fact, Atlantic Records was a large part of the story surrounding the eventual demise of Stax Records. Not only had Redding's death "devastated Stax…already on the verge of bankruptcy,"[161] but after a losing legal battle, Atlantic Records was given ownership and rights to the entire Redding catalog. A distribution conflict soon after with Columbia would serve as the last straw, and Stax folded soon after.

Redding's induction into the Rock & Roll Hall of Fame took place in 1989, and that same year, *Rolling Stone* voted him as the 89th greatest guitarist and the 7th greatest R&B artist of all time.

---

[160] Otis Redding, the King of Soul
[161] World News, Otis Redding Biography – www.wn.com/Otis-Redding

Having lived so few years, and with the heart of his professional career spanning less than a decade, more material than might be expected was available for posthumous compilations. A second volume of a live album from performances at Whisky A Go Go in Los Angeles came out in 1993, in addition to two volumes of "Greatest Hits" in the same year that the United States Postal Service introduced a commemorative Otis Redding stamp. No further complete compilation albums were released until 1998's "Dreams to Remember: The Very Best of Otis Redding." A year later, he received a Lifetime Achievement Grammy Award.

Despite dying at 26 and the obvious limits on quantity that his premature death entailed, Redding was not forgotten by the industry, and he never faded from the pantheon of public R&B heroes. Another compilation was released in 2002 as a joint album with Aretha Franklin, and in that year, Macon, Georgia erected a seven-foot high statue of Redding in Gateway Park. The Otis Redding Memorial Bridge now crosses the Ocmulgee River, "honoring its native son."[162]

[162] Star Pulse.com, Otis Redding Biography – www.starpulse.com/Music/Redding_Otis/Biography

Linda Cooley's picture of the Otis Redding statue

In 2003, *Rolling Stone* included five of Redding's recordings among the 500 greatest songs of all time, and the Stax Museum opened in Memphis on the first day of May, a facility which included a karaoke studio where guests could sing with Otis Redding for $15. In 2006, Johnny Jenkins, the eccentric guitarist who had made it all possible, died of a stroke, having failed to realize his original dreams after neglecting his collaborative assets with Redding as the latter grew in fame. Redding received the Legacy Award from the Rhythm and Blues Foundation in the same year.

To commemorate the 40th anniversary of Otis Redding's death, in 2007 and 2008 the Georgia Music Hall of Fame presented a major exhibition covering their native son's life, including a vast offering of music, photos, films, artifacts, hand-written lyrics, posters, and letters. The event was organized by the Otis Redding Foundation, managed under the careful direction of his family and estate.

Both traditional and off-beat tributes poured in after Redding's death and have continued to abound through the years. Barry Gibb has often said that the song "To Love Somebody" was written for Redding, but that he was never afforded the opportunity to record it. The Doors included references to Redding in their songs, and perhaps not unexpectedly, some of Jim Morrison's poetry is out of the ordinary: "Poor Otis is dead and gone, left me here to sing this song – pretty little girl with the red dress on – poor Otis dead and gone."[163]

2012 saw the passing of Donald "Duck" Dunn, a close colleague through the years who had always felt a special fondness for Redding. He was not able to see the 2013 documentary "Soul Ambassador", which was released and broadcast by the BBC Four. Its survey of Redding's career is comprehensive, "following [his life] from childhood and marriage to the Memphis studios and segregated southern clubs where he honed his unique stage act and voice."[164] Included are interviews with Redding's wife and daughter, in which Zelma states that "Otis enjoyed every minute of his life"[165] and noted that he was almost always "a glass-half-full person."[166]

Chapter 6: Redding's Legacy

Otis Redding was only one of a large number of artists who either purchased or chartered private planes to aid them with the logistics of touring and died in subsequent crashes, often in weather-related tragedies or from hiring deficient pilots. Likewise, he joins the thread of so many artists who died at a young age, swelling in number alongside those who were heavily involved in the drug culture and died of overdoses. As a perspective on how short a time Redding was able to pursue his professional plans, it is a telling reminder that he died "at a younger age than Jimi Hendrix, than Janis Joplin, than Brian Jones, than Jim Morrison."[167] Between the ages of 21 and 26, he produced 20 singles on the Billboard charts, and within the space of two years following his death, two more.

Although Otis Redding's music is, at its core, the traditional music of rural Georgia, his name will forever be synonymous with the blues-oriented city of Memphis, where Stax Records thrived for two decades before fading away due to catalog ownership and distribution conflicts

[163] Free Webs.com
[164] BBC Four, Otis Redding: Soul Ambassador – www.bbc.co.uk/programmes/b020tphg
[165] BBC Four, Otis Redding
[166] BBC Four, Otis Redding
[167] News 1, the Atlantic

with Atlantic and Columbia Records. Primarily owned by Jim Stewart and his specific musical preferences (not to mention a few peculiar rules regarding composition and orchestration), Stax gave Redding his first audition and then provided him with the space to develop a career that stood at the top of his industry for almost a decade. Within those few years, up to his untimely death in 1967, Redding went from roadie to musician, and then traveled around the country and Europe, all without appreciably changing the persona of his Southern genre. Rather than conform to overseas preferences, "he brought the music of his humble Georgia roots to the concert stages of Europe,"[168] drawing their ears into the authentic style of the Georgia sound instead of altering it for others' cultural expectations.

In order to properly understand the style in which Redding prospered, and the legacy left behind by his circle of artists, it is important to make distinctions between the various forms of "Soul" that came into being from such innovation and career expansiveness, beyond the general definition. Southern Soul can be defined as "today's extension of classic rhythm & blues from the 60s and 70s…[formatted in a] verse and chorus, story-telling tradition."[169] It borrows from country, gospel, rock, and pop. Less danceable, it is not just "the blues," and its best synonym is "country blues." Most of the music in the genre comes from the Deep South, but it is labeled thus because the music enjoys the greater popularity there.

The larger, generic body of "soul" music found itself being tailored into a variety of newly-labeled sub-genres during the 1950s, and Redding represented a blending of what was dubbed by various observers as Deep Soul, Southern Soul, Soul, and Soul Blues. Deep Soul is a sub-genre of Southern Soul, and insists on "an extreme adherence to soul's gospel roots."[170] This group of artists took gospel and "urbanized it, making it sleek and sprightly for upwardly mobile urban blacks."[171] The tempo and style is generally "slow and impassioned."[172] Soul Blues is a style of the 60s and 70s that combines soul and urban contemporary. Original inspirations came by way of artists such as fellow Macon native Little Richard, and Redding's vocal idol, the golden-voiced Sam Cooke, considered to be one of the greatest singer/songwriters to ever grace the American stage or recording studio. In the early years, spent in search of a vocal niche, Redding's first group of recordings, such as "Fat Gal" and "Shout Bamalama," tended more toward the "raw energy"[173] of Little Richard, but a listener could already hear homage to the "subtle grace of…Cooke."[174] Brought up in the classic forms, and as an admirer of Sam Cooke, Redding would base himself there, but at different times, he visited all of these forms in memorable tracks.

---

[168] Encyclopedia.com, Otis Redding – www.encyclopedia.com/topic/Otis_Redding.aspx

[169] Southern Soul RnB.com, What is Southern Soul? – www.southernsoulrnb.com/what-is-southern-soul.htm

[170] Robert Fontenot, About Entertainment, Oldies Music Glossary: Deep Soul – www.oldies.about.com/od/soulmotown/g/deepsoul.htm

[171] Robert Fontenot, About Entertainment

[172] Robert Fontenot, About Entertainment

[173] David Ritz, Encyclopaedia Britannica, Otis Redding – www.britannica.com/EBchecked/topic/494636/Otis-Redding

[174] David Ritz, Encyclopaedia Britannica

Over time, Redding would come to enjoy the same sort of admiration Sam Cooke had, despite their dissimilarities in vocal and visual performance styles. Cooke, who was shot to death in 1964, was known for an inordinately "sincere emotional delivery,"[175] which came to be reflected in Redding's offerings as well. Redding clearly used Cooke as a model, and though Redding "lacked the virtuosity" of Cooke, both men had "flawless musical taste and musical intellect,"[176] despite a musical education that could be described as nothing more than rustic. This type of informal (and in many ways incomplete) musical upbringing served as the antithesis of Motown's preference for advanced studio technology and harmonic sophistication displayed by such artists as Marvin Gaye and Stevie Wonder. For Stax, this all but guaranteed the purity of the original form, as found in the rural roots of Redding's Georgia, without the extravagant instrumental enhancement and peripheral elaboration. Redding could not name the chord or give a formal analysis of the melodic structure, but he found a way to produce them anyway through great effort and natural gifts.

In live performances, Redding has been described by important critics as having a "magnetic stage presence and sincerity,"[177] which in a sense stands in stark contrast with what he was like in real life. When the mood was right, his style of delivery could be volcanic and frenzied, and his output of energy was labeled by one biographer as "incendiary," but he was also an "intricate and deeply cerebral singer,"[178] and his greatest gift, all things taken into account, "may have been his command and understatement."[179] If anything, Redding brought a spontaneity to live performance that even he could not describe or explain, barely aware at times how he had just performed at all. Critic Dave Marsh once commented that a typical Redding performance "sounds as though each line is coming to him only the instant before he sings it,"[180] a reflection of just how in the moment Redding was when he was on the spot and underneath the lights.

Despite the turbulent nature of the 1960s, Otis Redding was not only comfortable with collaboration between the races but believed that such a state of cooperation must exist, both in life and in music. Intentionally assembling a band of mixed races, in keeping with the credo of Stax Records, he was hailed on one hand for his sense of enlightenment and progressive outlook, but he was also criticized for not actively participating in certain aspects of the Civil Rights Movement, particularly by those of a more militant mindset. Dogmatic members of the cause often accused Redding of being inauthentic, but as an artist, he seemed unperturbed by such commentary.

Despite the overwhelming power of his on-stage persona, Redding is remembered by family and colleagues as a quiet, thoughtful man with an excellent sense of humor who had few axes to

[175] Bio.com, Otis Redding Biography – www.biography.com/people/otis-redding-9453430#synopsis
[176] News 1, "The Songs Otis Redding Could Have Sung", in *The Atlantic* – www.otisredding.com/anything_slides-1
[177] Bio.Com, Otis Redding Biography
[178] News 1, the Atlantic
[179] News 1, the Atlantic
[180] News 1, the Atlantic

grind with anyone. Compared many artists suddenly thrust into the limelight of an international music career, his life remained surprisingly scandal-free, unlike Sam Cooke, and he was much more the family man than other hard-partying adoration seekers in the industry. Similarly well-disposed toward colleagues, his sometimes whimsical sense of humor can be heard in tongue-in-cheek songs such as "Fat Gal" and "Tramp," and when another artist's cover of his song hit the big time, as did Aretha Franklin's rendition of "Respect," Redding suffered no emotional bruises from her success. When asked, he jokingly replied, "That little girl stole my song!"[181]

In terms of a purely vocal sound, pinning down Redding has never been an easy task. Listening to the Monterey Festival rendition of "Shake," listeners can hear a prime example of the chainsaw-like vocal burn that has always been popular as a special effect in non-classical vocal music. Redding, however, could make it an exciting staple and never let it slip out of control, as so often occurs with prolonged use. At the opposite end of the spectrum, however, are his renditions of songs such as "These Arms of Mine," in which the rough edges are pulled back and replaced by an alluring sweetness housed within a quick, youthful vibrato (the rhythmic oscillation of the vocal cords). In addition, he borrowed the gift of singing slightly off the beat from the jazz world, adding "gruff, syncopated reflections to ballad and uptempo material."[182] This ability to play with and around the beat, *swinging*, loosened the beat-oriented personality of the form over time.

While the Motown preference was generally directed toward the higher tenor voice, Redding, although certainly not a deep bass or bass-baritone, could carry a slightly deeper, more resonant acoustic than Michael Jackson, Marvin Gaye, or Stevie Wonder. Some historians have claimed that Motown's love of higher voices was predicated on the lessened fear of a perceived sexual aggression broadcast to female listeners, but regardless of that theory's veracity, Redding's greater accessibility to fuller resonance when called for, combined with his overtly sexualized lyrics, made a powerful recipe. Furthermore, the raw nature of the music and its popularity suggested that female listeners embraced Redding all the same, so he clearly didn't need the musical etiquette and protection offered by Motown refinement. In live appearances, Redding's 6'2, 220 pound physique only added to the intensity of the atmosphere.

Given his good-tempered nature, Redding would very likely have been more complimented by the covers of his songs and their subsequent popularity than he would have been by various honors like the Grammy Lifetime Achievement Award, the Rock & Roll Hall of Fame, the Songwriters Hall of Fame, and the enduring nickname "The King of Soul." Over 45 years after his death, Redding's music has been covered by seemingly every possible kind of musician, including Bob Dylan, The Grateful Dead, Willie Nelson, Al Green, Pearl Jam, John Mayer, Christine Aguilera, Etta James, Rod Stewart, Kanye West, and even Mae West.[183] The extreme

---

[181] News 1, the Atlantic

[182] Rock & Roll Hall of Fame, Otis Redding Biography

[183] Museum of American Soul Music, Otis Redding – www.staxmuseum.com/about/artists/view/otis-redding

diversity of artists who took up Redding's music as an inspiration speaks not only to its universality but to its professional versatility, as many of the songs, most notably "(Sittin' On) The Dock of the Bay," seem to succeed in almost any style, vocal range, or halfway thought-out arrangement.

Given the argument over Redding's place within the context of the Civil Rights movement, Redding is often compared to Sam Cooke, but he is also juxtaposed with Jimi Hendrix, who was so popular among hippies. David Ritz, critic and historian, points out that the "radical heroes went both ways, and not just for the money."[184] Ritz falls firmly on the side of Redding's integrity, recalling that "you'll see Otis singing (and singing as beautifully as I've ever heard him), charming a white hippie audience…what Otis is doing is giving of himself, and his music, sharing."[185]

Countless critics, historians, and listeners insist that "playing up to whitey"[186] is the one thing Redding was not doing, a notion entertained by fellow critic Brian Ward in a minority opinion. Ward makes the claim that Redding and Hendrix were "accepted across ethnic lines because they were engaged in minstrelsy."[187] Biographer Guralnick disagrees, asserting that Hendrix was not accepted among members of his own race because his was generally a hippie audience, not an oppressed black one. Redding, in contrast, took a mostly pure version of his race's rural music to the region, the country, and the world without changing its basic nature for a white audience, whether American or European. In this way, he brought the international audience to himself and his music, rather than the other way around.[188]

One need only look at the integrity of Redding's music to see the reflection of the same integrity in his career. 26 years old at the time of his death, he seemed much older to many "because he had perfect taste and a disregard for fashion – he never confused expressiveness with frenzy,"[189] at least not in his mature years. He was forever searching for a way to "transcend the artifice of a song,"[190] the highest calling of any vocal interpreter in all classical and non-classical genres. In matters of performance style, "none of the [vocal] effects he achieved were gratuitous,"[191] and his masterful ability to sing "in subtle opposition to the beat,"[192] was a vehicle of artistic exploration rather than a self-serving signature statement.

---

[184] David Ritz, "Happy Song: Soul Music in the Ghetto", in *Salmagundi*, No. 12, Spring, 1970, Skidmore College

[185] David Ritz, *Salmagundi*

[186] Brian Ward, "Just My Soul Responding: Rhythm and Blues, Black Consciousness, and Race Relations", Review by Clyde Woods, in *The Georgia Historical Quarterly*, Vol. 83, No. 4, Winter, 1999

[187] Brian Ward, *Georgia Historical Quarterly*

[188] Christopher Bello, The Harvard Crimson, the Death of Otis Redding, Jan. 11, 1968 – www.thecrimson.com/article/1968/1/11/the-death-of-otis-redding-ptho

[189] Christopher Bello, The Harvard Crimson

[190] Christopher Bello, The Harvard Crimson

[191] Christopher Bello, The Harvard Crimson

[192] Christopher Bello, The Harvard Crimson

Zelma Redding, the woman closest to Otis, has zealously defended the positive characterizations of his intentions and his personal and artistic honesty. Among her interviews and written recollections, she suggests that Redding "was such a humble person and so appreciated what was going on."[193] In particular, she took strong exception to Scott Freeman's biography of her husband, a work she refers to as "a no good book"[194] that she arranged to have banned from the Georgia Music Hall of Fame. Indeed, in lieu of riches, power, popularity, or false images, Zelma's core belief is one that might be shared by a great many listeners and devotees worldwide: "I always thought everything he sang, he sang to me."[195]

Marvin Gaye

Chapter 1: Troubled Childhood

"If you cannot find peace within yourself, you will never find it anywhere else." – Marvin Gaye

Marvin Pentz Gay, Jr. was born at Freedman Hospital in Washington, D.C. on April 2, 1939, and he grew up in the segregated Deanwood section of the city. Ironically, his mother, Alberta Cooper, was a domestic worker from Rocky Mount, North Carolina who had once witnessed her father shooting her mother in an argument. Gaye, his name not yet ending with "e" (which he later added to avoid teasing and widespread violence in the neighborhood, and as a way of emulating his hero, Sam Cooke), took solace in music as a child, an outlet that at least partially served as protection from his father, who was born in 1914 as one of 15 children in a violent environment. Attaching himself to a spin-off sect of the Seventh Day Adventist Church, Marvin Gay, Sr. established a modest reputation as a healer, and by the time he had children, he had risen to become a minister in a church that defined itself by fusing together elements of orthodox beliefs, Judaism, and Pentacostalism, maintaining a severe code of theological and personal conduct, and celebrating no traditional holidays common to other denominations.

During Marvin's childhood, the family established membership in the House of God, and as an opponent of "sparing the rod" in even the most minor incidents, Marvin, his brother Frankie, and his sisters Jeanne and Zeola were beaten on an almost daily basis. Biblical "quizzes" took place in the Gay home with regularity, and incorrect answers were rewarded with severe whippings. Marvin himself later discussed how the family observed Sabbath: "We kept the Sabbath in the purest sense. Father anointed converts with olive oil and baptized them in the river. The Sabbath was his day, it was God's day, and it was also a day for singing. Every member was blessed with a good voice. The joy of music was the joy of God."

[193] John Ballon, Must Hear.com, Otis Redding and Jimi Hendrix – www.musthear.com/music/reviews/otis-redding-and-jimi-hendrix/live-at-the-Monterey-international-pop-festival/
[194] Jack Barlow, *Salon*, "Otis Redding's Widow," Aug. 18, 2013 – www.salon.com/2013/08/otis-reddings-widow-i-always-thought-that-everything-he-sang-he-sang-for-me"
[195] Jack Barlow, *Salon*

As these episodes suggest, Marvin, Sr., a one-time postal and Western Union clerk before rising to local prominence in the church, has been described by rock historians as "a terminally out of work fundamentalist preacher…[who] ranted against the sins of indulgence…yet he was an avid consumer of vodka, and was a zealous cross-dresser."[196] Another child from one of Alberta's previous relationships was sent away, as Marvin, Sr. could not, by his own admission, bear to raise another man's child, and Alberta confided on more than one occasion that he harbored a simmering hatred for Marvin, Jr. as well. In fact, Marvin, Sr. often claimed that the son who bore his name was actually the child of another man, and according to Alberta, "My husband never wanted Marvin, and he never liked him. He used to say he didn't think he was really his child. I told him that was nonsense. He knew Marvin was his. But for some reason, he didn't love Marvin, and what's worse, he didn't want me to love Marvin either. Marvin wasn't very old before he understood that."

For his part, Gaye believed that his father got some sort of sadistic pleasure out of beating him. He once told author David Ritz, "It wasn't simply that my father beat me though that was bad enough. By the time I was twelve, there wasn't an inch on my body that hadn't been bruised and beaten by him." In addition to his belief that his father "was enjoying the whole thing," Gaye explained that he was forced to anticipate an imminent beating by being forced to listen to his father crack his belt loudly. It was bad enough that Marvin claimed "if it wasn't for Mother, who was always there to console me and praise me for my singing, I think I would have been one of those child suicide cases you read about in the papers."

While he was obviously more than stern, Marvin, Sr. also claimed to be attracted to "soft things," which included appearing around the house wearing his wife's clothing, a constant point of deep humiliation for his son. To put it mildly, Marvin Gay, Sr. "embodied a rather complicated model of morality,"[197] but a more overt analysis might characterize him as "a solitary, violent man"[198] who, according to Alberta Cooper Gay, was filled with "envy over his son's tremendous success."[199] This jealousy over his son's accomplishments would add further ire to the inordinate and abnormal hatred that was always present in Gaye's childhood. In addition to being beaten, Jeanne is rumored to have been sexually molested by another family member as well.

It was the intention of Marvin Sr. from the very beginning that his son would take up a religious vocation. Since secular music was forbidden in the house, and considering Marvin's natural instinct to make music, it was understandable that he would sing and play in the church environment. In addition to coaching at the piano with his father, described by family members

---

[196] David Krajicek, Crime Library, The Life and Death of Marvin Gaye –
www.crimelibrary.com/notorious_murders/celebrity/marvin_gaye/index.html

[197] This Day in History, Marvin Gaye is shot and killed by his own father – www.history.com/this-day-in-history/marvin-gaye-is-shot-and-killed-by-his-own-father

[198] Classic Bands.com, Marvin Gaye – www.classicbands.com/gaye.html

[199] This Day in History

as the only peaceful period between the two in their entire lives, Gaye started singing in church rallies from the age of 5. However, when the House of God opted not to select Gay, Sr. as Chief Apostle, the family left the church and Marvin's father descended deeper and deeper into a chronic alcoholic state.

Despite his surroundings, Marvin continued in church music and gained increasing proficiency on organ and piano. Of course, as anyone who has ever heard one of his songs knows, Gaye also developed what would become an extraordinary singing voice during his high school years. It was during high school that he fell in love with music genres never heard at home, and he developed a particular fondness for R&B and doo-wop. After working with several local groups, he joined The Marquees, a band that performed mostly for high school audiences. Under the direction of Harvey Fuqua, The Marquees would eventually become Harvey and the New Moonglows, as well as Gaye's ticket out of Washington, D.C. and the restrictive environment of home.

The Moonglows in 1956

Chapter 2: Escape to Motown

"Music, not sex, got me aroused." – Marvin Gaye

Gaye's musical activities obviously could not have sat well with his father, but his ventures into the outer world came more quickly than he might have expected. Gay, Sr. kicked his son out of the house promptly after he dropped out of high school, but once he began working as a dishwasher, young Gaye felt the humiliation of menial work keenly. As an alternative, he enlisted in the Air Force and entertained thoughts of becoming a pilot, but he ended up in the same demeaning situation, washing dishes, peeling potatoes, and being allowed nowhere near a military aircraft.

In fact, it was during military service that the full force of Gaye's rebellion emerged, and he refused to follow orders at every turn. Following a protracted attempt to feign mental illness, he was eventually discharged, and although the official record listed it as honorable, the accompanying notes noted his "refusal to follow orders...Marvin Gaye cannot adjust to regimentation and authority."[200] Before he left, however, Gaye had been introduced to sex in ways that he never even knew existed. In addition to losing his virginity to a prostitute, he described the Air Force as "a world of pure sex where people turned off their minds and fed their lusts, no questions asked. The concept sickened me, but I also found it exciting."

Gaye had scarcely taken off his uniform before he was already working with a number of "street corner doo-wop groups"[201] upon his return to Washington, D.C. The Rainbows were a local attraction, and Gaye received mentoring at the hands of Bo Diddley before recording a single, "Wyatt Earp" on the Okeh label. This caught the attention of Harvey Fuqua, whose Marquees, now performing as The Moonglows, were heading north so that Fuqua, along with girlfriend Gwen Gordy of the Motown family, could establish his own record company in the same neighborhood as the major powers of the industry. Not at all sorry to live at a greater distance from his father, Gaye went north with the Moonglows, and in 1959, he toured with them as part of the backup band. Gaye can also be heard prominently on the band's hit single "Ten Commandments of Love." However, his revulsion to touring was instant, and he described his first outing with The Moonglows as "an unpleasant, eye-opening experience."[202]

[200] David Ritz, Marvin Gaye Biography, Sing365.com – www.sing365.com/lyric.nsf/Marvin-Gaye-Biography/2479E1513170C15348256BD400117645
[201] Jason Ankeny, All Music
[202] Classic Bands.com

Masao Nakagami's picture of Bo Diddley performing in Japan

Despite how much he hated touring, Gaye ended up in Detroit with Fuqua and his group, and in that same year, he recorded a series of singles for a fledgling record company called Chess. The track for "Mama Loocie" marked the first time he recorded as a lead singer, and by 1960, Gaye was working good hours as a session drummer, albeit for only five dollars per week. While the pay was low, Gaye was working with top-of-the-line performers and recording artists like Smokey Robinson and the Miracles, Stevie Wonder, the Supremes, the Marvelettes, and Martha and the Vandellas, all artists working with a subsidiary label for Motown called the Anna label.

Gaye met Berry Gordy at a Christmas party where Gaye sang and played, and Gordy was so impressed that he signed Gaye to another of the subsidiaries, Tamla Records, where he was given his first ongoing opportunities to work as a vocalist with the single "Let Your Conscience Be Your Guide." However, this, and other early efforts, fell somewhat off the mark, and finding the right place for Gaye's vocal sound and style quickly became a faltering experiment. Vocally capable as he was, Gaye, in the beginning, "struggled to find his voice"[203] in terms of genre, and he didn't help matters much by resisting Motown's attempts to shape him in any way. For example, the John Roberts Powers School for Social Grace in Detroit required a course offered by Maxine Powell, and her course was all but mandatory for Motown artists, but Gaye flatly

---

[203] Jason Ankeny, All Music

refused to participate and demonstrated no interest in the studio's call for uniform behavior and consistent public image. Powell was at least able to convince him, however, that he should sing with his eyes open, observing, "It looks you're sleeping when you're performing."[204]

Angela George's picture of Barry Gordy

Through the early '60s, Gaye continued as a session musician while Motown tried to figure out what to do with him. He supplied the drum tracks for the iconic "Please Mr. Postman," written by the Marvelettes, but the most important association for Gaye at the time was his increasing attraction to Gordy's sister, Anna. Their relationship all but guaranteed him a path to new opportunities with Motown, including the production of his first album designed for the "club singer" audience. *The Soulful Moods of Marvin Gaye* was a collection of "low-key, smooth ballads with a jazz feel,"[205] but given that Anna was 17 years Marvin's senior, not to mention the fact she was a record executive, composer, and songwriter, many accused Gaye of romancing his way to the top. The couple had met while Gaye was with The Moonglows, and Anna would share writing credits for some of Gaye's future efforts.

1962 brought Gaye his first inklings that he could make hits with the aptly named "Stubborn

---

[204] R&B Hall of Fame, Marvin Gaye
[205] Encyclopedia.com, Gaye, Marvin – www.encyclopedia.com/topic/Marvin_Gaye.aspx

Kind of Fellow," which reached the number 8 spot on R&B charts. In addition to that, "Hitch Hike" and "Pride and Joy" also did well; "Hitch Hike" was Gaye's first top 40 solo single, and "Pride and Joy" was his first top 10. Once "Pride and Joy" brought Gaye some prosperity, he moved his parents to a better neighborhood and provided his mother with enough money to stop working. Despite insinuations that Gaye was using Anna, he said "Pride and Joy" was written about her: "When I composed 'Pride and Joy', I was head over heels in love with Anna. I just wrote what I felt about her, and what she did for me. She was my pride and joy."

Throughout the early part of the decade, Gaye churned out a steady stream of dance music, scoring with "Can I Get a Witness," which was written by Brian Holland, Lamont Dozier, and Eddie Holland and reached number 22 on the pop charts. These early recordings clearly reflected Gaye's musical background, featuring "a churchiness…that was pushed by that urgent Detroit rhythm section."[206] Dividing his time between session work and solo recording, he worked as the drummer for the Stevie Wonder hit "Fingertips, pt. 2," and he co-wrote with Martha & the Vandellas for 1962's "Beachwood 4-5789" and 1964's "Dancing in the Street," which ended up being that group's biggest hit.

Chapter 3: Duets

"I hope to refine music, study it, try to find some area that I can unlock. I don't quite know how to explain it but it's there. These can't be the only notes in the world, there's got to be other notes some place, in some dimension, between the cracks on the piano keys." – Marvin Gaye

Gaye had a hand in some of Motown's biggest records of the era, but they were mostly for other artists, and when it came to his solo career, Gaye protested that the songs handed to him were too far above the top of his vocal range. He already felt self-conscious about being a tenor, and he further believed that the high voice quality didn't fit with his image. He often complained of being the puppet of the three figures of authority in his life - Berry, Anna, and Motown – and even as "Pride and Joy" had become a hit in 1963, Gaye's insistence on recording slow ballads in the older "club" style continued. That itch was at least partly satisfied when Motown began to pair him with the best female singers on the artist roster, and combined the suave aspects of his phrasing style with complementary soprano voices. This soothed some of Gaye's complaints, and despite his rigid stances on some points, he was "popular and well-liked around Motown…[and] carried himself in a sophisticated, gentlemanly manner," which suggests he might not have needed Ms. Powell's course to understand in-studio etiquette.

Mary Wells, Gaye's first serious duet partner, was a pioneer in shaping the studio's public sound, and she had been described by Gordy himself as the "First Lady" of Motown. The already Grammy-nominated artist had recently scored with an enormous and lasting hit, "My Guy," by the time she began her work with Gaye. 1964 saw the production and release of *Together*, a

---

[206] Star Pulse.com, Marvin Gaye Biography – www.starpulse.com/music/Gaye_Marvin/Biography/

collection of their duets that also happened to be Gaye's first charting album. Wells and Gaye continued with a string of successful singles, including "Once Upon a Time," and "What's the Matter with You, Baby?"

Mary Wells

With his newfound fame heightened, Gaye suddenly found himself a favorite of the entertainment media, which allowed him to appear on television venues such as American Bandstand, Shindig, Hullabaloo, and the Mike Douglas Show. He received top billing in the Motown Revue and appeared in *TAMI*, a concert film, with the Beach Boys, Chuck Berry, the Rolling Stones, James Brown, and others. The 1964 duets also assured Gaye of his first international success, as he appeared that year on the London-based television program *Ready, Steady, Go!*

Gaye followed up 1964 with three top 10 hits in 1965: "Ain't That Peculiar," "I'll Be

Doggone," and "How Sweet It Is (To Be Loved By You)." "How Sweet It Is (To Be Loved By You)" has been an enduring hit that is still instantly recognizable over a generation later, and it was also proof of Motown's success as a whole. Demonstrating a magic touch for hit singles, 39 out of the 40 released by Motown would eventually reach the top ten, many of which Gaye himself wrote and/or arranged. Such success caused Motown to loosen the reins of artistic control, and in the following months, Gaye was even allowed to record a collection of Broadway show tunes. Through this constant experimentation with their new star, however, Motown came to realize that the public liked Gaye best as an R&B singer, a market in which he could be presented to the public as a ladies' man and a great duet singer surrounded by beautiful and talented female artists.

Promo shot of Gaye for "Ain't That Peculiar"

Committing itself to that new course of action, Motown provided Gaye's second important partnership in the form of Kim Weston, and together, they recorded the duet album *It Takes Two*. This was the most successful of Gaye's collaborations to that point, and it helped cement him as "one of the era's dominant duet singers."[207] The partnership might have gone on to greater

---

[207] Jason Ankeny, All Music

things, but soon after the release, and with further plans in the offing, Weston left Motown over a royalty dispute with Gordy. Subsequent attempts at sustaining her career proved less than successful.

Kim Weston

Despite losing Weston, the best was yet to come for Gaye when it came to duets. The third partnership Gaye had was with Tammi Terrell, one of the era's brightest Motown stars, and according to the vast majority of listeners and critics, this was definitely Gaye's most successful partnership if not Motown's as a whole. Tracks such as "Ain't No Mountain High Enough," "Ain't Nothin' Like the Real Thing," and "You're All I Need to Get By" were instant hits, and the duo would go on to record seven top 40 singles. At first, the duets were recorded in separate studios and remixed without the artists working directly together, but it soon became apparent that such an approach was unnecessary. Terrell and Gaye began to perform live, something Gaye had never enjoyed, but with Terrell, he now approached it with a new confidence. The relationship between the two is said to have been entirely platonic, which was confirmed by Gaye himself, but he also admitted that once she began to sing, no one could have been more in love with her than he was during those sessions. Officially, Terrell was in a relationship with

David Ruffin of The Temptations, but Gaye thought the world of her, regardless of their degree of intimacy.

Tammi Terrell

Many of the greatest hits performed by Gaye and Terrell were written by the team of Nikolas Ashford and Valerie Simpson, who would later co-write "What's Going On" with Gaye. Simpson assisted with Terrell's vocals in later releases, and the writing team remained one of Gaye's important professional associations.

The collaboration's success increased steadily through 1967, but Terrell began to complain of numerous bouts with migraines, and while performing with Gaye at a homecoming celebration for Hampton-Sydney College in Virginia, she collapsed on stage into his arms. Subsequent exams revealed a brain tumor, and after eight unsuccessful operations, Terrell retired from live performing in 1969 after recording "You're All I Need to Get By" from a wheelchair.

Chapter 4: What's Going On

"With the world exploding around me, how am I supposed to keep singing love songs?" – Marvin Gaye

In 1968, Gaye experienced the pinnacle of his solo work up to that time in "I Heard It Through the Grapevine." The single sold four million copies over a fairly brief period after its release, and it maintain the number 1 spot for a stretch of seven consecutive weeks. That same year, Marvin had four hits, two of them recorded with Terrell, in the U.S. top ten, and by 1969, "Grapevine" was an international sensation, not only for Gaye's own rendition but because of a more up-tempo version recorded by Gladys Knight & the Pips. It has remained popular ever since, and it is even associated with a vast marketing campaign for a cereal company using now famous animated raisins. Regardless of Gaye's disdain for the popularity of "I Heard it On the Grapevine," rock critic Dave Marsh, in his book *The Heart of Rock & Roll: The Hundred Greatest Singles Ever Made*, "deemed it the best single ever recorded."[208] For his part, Gaye did not revel in the single's success, despite its marketing and financial rewards, because he felt it was undeserved. His own recording of the Norman Whitfield, Barrett Strong song was described by one critic as a "dejected, paranoid reading,"[209] distinctly contrasted by the "fiery treatment" offered by Gladys Knight.

Gaye in 1968

Other problems troubled Gaye's personal life at the time. In addition to the precarious medical condition of Tammi Terrell, his marriage with Anna, now into its sixth year, was crumbling, and

[208] Encyclopedia.com, Marvin Gaye
[209] Rolling Stone Artists

frequent explosive arguments in public between the two could not help but be noticed. There were widespread allegations of domestic abuse on both their parts, and Gaye would ruefully note, "Marriage is miserable unless you find the right person that is your soulmate and that takes a lot of looking."

Despite having a few hits in 1969, including "Too Busy Thinking About My Baby," and "That's the Way Love Is," Gaye was in no condition to enjoy his success. In addition to troubles with Anna, Tammi Terrell, who had become a "beloved partner,"[210] had her health gradually deteriorate due to brain cancer and the inability to manage her condition successfully, despite an attempted 8 surgeries. Terrell and Gaye had enjoyed three "high-flying"[211] years of duet hits, but in the final recording sessions, many of her vocals had to be covered by Valerie Simpson for the release of *Easy*. When she died in March 1970 at just 24 years old, it was the most devastating blow to strike Gaye yet. Not only did Gaye give the eulogy, he was the only one associated with Motown who was even welcome at the funeral.

Consumed with turmoil, there was a serious increase in Gaye's cocaine use, which contributed to the general darkness of his life over the next year. During that time, he went into seclusion and all but abandoned music, and even when he wasn't completely down in the dumps, he swore that he would never again work with a female singer. At times, he threatened to quit for good. Casting about for something with which to occupy his time, something that would take his attention off of his loss, Gaye even sought to try out for the Detroit Lions football team, going so far as to befriend star athletes Mel Farr and Lem Barney. The danger to his career, however, was judged as being too great, so the tryout was suspended.

By the time he finally decided to re-emerge, Terrell's absence had left him in a more mindful state about his own goals and aspirations. Gaye's customary resistance to being shaped and monitored came back all the more fiercely in his decision to join other artists of his generation in the protest movement, which would see him make increasingly social and political statements in his music.

Gaye's new resolve after returning to Motown was, to him, beyond argument, even when pressure came from the CEO of the studio himself. *What's Going On*, Gaye's 11th studio album, was completed on May 21, 1971, containing not just the legendary title track but also "God is Love" and an early version of "Flyin' High (In the Friendly Sky). Gaye himself supervised the production of the album with long hours spent in a marijuana smoke-filled studio in one of Motown's facilities. With alcohol in abundance as well, Gaye manned the piano, with "Pistol" Allen on drums, while an exceedingly drunk and inspired James Jamerson played bass, laying down some of the best tracks of his career.

---

[210] Bio.com, Marvin Gaye Biography – www.biography.com/people/marvin-gaye-9307988
[211] Bio.com, Marvin Gaye Biography

As a single, the song "What's Going On" would go on to become Motown's fastest-selling record, and the album as a whole was listed among the top 10 albums of the year by TIME Magazine, but it was a struggle just to get the album released. In the album, Gaye overturned the "feel good" Motown message, and erupted with commentary on all of society's pet peeves, from Vietnam, racism, poverty and pollution to political corruption. Among the most powerful triggers for such an emergence was the killing of students at Kent State University by members of the National Guard. Taking over the studio himself to record the album with complete artistic control, Gaye broke every rule in the Motown rule book, but not without a fight. "His fingerprints were all over every element of the recording,"[212] but the album's release, at least this time, was on hold pending Berry Gordy's verdict, and a shocked Gordy flatly refused. When Gaye told Gordy he wanted to do a protest song, Gordy replied, "Marvin, don't be ridiculous. That's taking things too far." In fact, when Gaye played Gordy the title song, Gordy told him it was "the worst thing I ever heard in my life."

To say that *What's Going On* clashed with Motown's idea of "creative direction"[213] goes beyond understatement. Gaye had produced an album so at odds with the studio's projected image of him, and so far from the place where they believed he could be the most effective, that Gordy barely knew how to respond. Compared to Gaye's former work, *What's Going On* was a "highly percussive album that incorporated jazz and classical elements…a remarkably sophisticated and fluid soul sound…[from] deeply held spiritual beliefs."[214] Along with all the other social ills, Gaye expressed vicarious impressions of Vietnam through the letters sent by his brother Frankie from the war. In short, there was scarcely a Motown "feel good" moment in the entire collection.

Gordy's refusal to release the album was accompanied by vehemently overt and distinct opinions. It was, according to him, too jazz-oriented, too outdated in its musical references to former eras, and far too political. He reserved a particular hatred for the "Dizzie Gillespie-styled scats."[215] Baffled by the album's general thrust and tone of personality, Gordy remarked that he could never understand the intention of the album's full scope or where it came from, and he expressed a fear that such a release would cause the "ruination of Gaye's image as a sex symbol."[216] The decision was emphatic and final: *What's Going On* would never be released by Motown Records.

An epic stalemate between the record company and Gaye, its star singer, ensued, the magnitude of which had to be entirely unexpected by Gordy, who completely underestimated Gaye's capacity for stubbornness. Believing in the work he had produced, and the first album for

---

[212] Encyclopedia.com, Marvin Gaye

[213] Bio.com, Marvin Gaye

[214] Jason Ankeny, All Music

[215] SOS, Sound on Sound, Marvin Gaye, "What's Going On" – Classical Tracks – www.soundonsound.com/sos/jul11/articles/classic-tracks-0711.htm

[216] SOS, Sound on Sound, Marvin Gaye

which he would eventually receive producer credits at that, Gaye simply refused to sing another note for Motown and stuck to his guns. The standoff lasted several months, with an irate Gordy seeking out every avenue of influence he could find to coax or force Gaye into relenting and returning to work. One such avenue was Smokey Robinson, who convinced the executive that Marvin Gaye would hold his position until doomsday, and that the studio might as well give up on any thoughts of wearing him down or reaching a compromise.

Dwight McCann's picture of Smokey Robinson

Ultimately, an aggravated Gordy allowed the printing of 100,000 copies, a token number at best, but he was still caught completely by surprise when the entire pressing sold out within 24 hours. In shock, the potential for profit changed everything, so naturally, Gordy "was placated"[217] immediately. Sure enough, the public responded positively to *What's Going On* in an instant, and Gaye was receiving awards from the NAACP before another disc could be taken off the press, despite the fact that Gordy had commissioned another album to cash in on the success. Eventual sales of "What's Going On" would reach over 2.5 million for the single, while the album would go on to become the first million-unit seller on its way to being named Album of the Year. A buoyed Gaye even took to the live stage again at the Kennedy Center before signing a new million dollar contract with Motown, the most lucrative for any black artist at the time. In a very real sense, Gaye had "articulated his own declaration of independence in 1971 – now he would produce himself, singing his own songs, setting his own agenda."[218]

The title song, "What's Going On," that so famously headlined Gaye's 11th studio album, found its origins long before Gaye started the album. Renaldo "Obie" Benson of The Four Tops had written the song after witnessing a severe case of police brutality at a Vietnam protest in San Francisco. Benson noted of the song's origins, "I saw this and started wondering 'what the heck was going on, what is happening here?' One question led to another. Why are they sending kids so far away from their families overseas? Why are they attacking their own children in the streets?" Contrary to the belief that the song was a protest against Vietnam, Benson explained, "My partners told me it was a protest song. I said 'no man, it's a love song, about love and understanding. I'm not protesting, I want to know what's going on.'"

[217] SOS, Sound on Sound
[218] David Ritz, Marvin Gaye Biography

Arnie Lee's picture of Obie Benson

Although Benson introduced the concept for consideration, The Four Tops were hesitant to touch anything with such an incendiary topic, so the song sat around for awhile. Later, it was offered to Joan Baez, who never shied away from a troubling issue, but the connection was never made, so the song remained unrecorded. Gaye himself originally thought it'd be better to let another group record the song, but Benson ultimately convinced him to perform the song himself.

In the end, Gaye stepped in to do the song, and in discussing that song and the album as a whole, he remarked, "In 1969 or 1970, I began to re-evaluate my whole concept of what I wanted my music to say.... I was very much affected by letters my brother was sending me from Vietnam, as well as the social situation here at home. I realized that I had to put my own fantasies behind me if I wanted to write songs that would reach the souls of people. I wanted them to take a look at what was happening in the world."[219] Gaye's ongoing attention to the issue, the deeply-felt empathy with his brother's letters, and witnesses to the recording process indicate that *What's Going On* was in no way an irrational or hastily assembled concept but a deliberate and single-minded long-term goal. Ken Sands, one of Motown's recording engineers on the project, remembered those days in the studio fondly: "One thing that I'll say about Marvin is that he was always kind...forceful in terms of what he wanted...but also a very sweet and gentle man who treated people calmly."[220]

The text for the title track begins with "Father, father (we don't need to escalate)," but in a later version, it was changed to "Mother, mother," based perhaps on Gaye's negative feelings toward his father. Others would describe it as a "burning hatred for his father and eternal love for his mother."[221] Either way, the release of the "What's Going On" single in 1971, in addition to the album, brought a new audience to Gaye's music without noticeably sacrificing any segment of the old one, and the album brought widespread acclaim as Rolling Stone's Album of the Year. Benson gave enormous credit to Gaye, saying he "added some things that were more ghetto, more natural, which made it seem like a story than a song...we measured him for the suit and he tailored the hell out of it."

Gaye himself considered the entire concept and result as a gift from God, and two follow-ups, "Mercy Mercy Me (The Ecology)" and "Inner City Blues (Make Me Wanna Holler)" both reached the top ten and brought Gaye an even greater degree of artistic clout within the studio. The end of "Inner City Blues" features a segment that serves as a prelude to "What's Going On" but also as a reprise in the total flow of the album, indicating strong relationships between everything Gaye was creating in this phase of his career. The reprise was eliminated from the original pressings, but it has been restored in later versions. As singles, "Mercy Mercy Me" and "Inner City Blues" both reached number 2.

Critiquing the overall album, in which all the parts bear important text and tonal relationships to one another, Britain's Q Magazine observed that *What's Going On* "did for soul what Blonde on Blonde and Sgt. Pepper had done for rock, [through its] darkly atmospheric, jazzy sound."[222] , The critic for *Rolling Stone* at the time said of the album, "Ambitious, personal albums may be a glut on the market elsewhere, but at Motown they're something new... the album as a whole takes

---

[219] SOS, Sound on Sound
[220] Bio.com, Marvin Gaye
[221] IMDb, Marvin Gaye Biography – www.imdb.com/name/nm0310848/nio?ref_=nm_ov_bio
[222] Rock & Roll Hall of Fame

precedence, absorbing its own flaws. There are very few performers who could carry a project like this off. I've always admired Marvin Gaye, but I didn't expect that he would be one of them. Guess I seriously underestimated him. It won't happen again." Focusing on the "shattered American dream of the early 1970s,"[223] it is, in hindsight, highly esteemed as "a sublimely soulful piece of social commentary."[224]

Chapter 5: At the Top?

"I am not a star. At least, I don't consider myself a star." – Marvin Gaye

1971 was an enormous year for Gaye, but life outside the studio went on, and the year was crowded with other events as well. This was the year in which he began an affair with Janis Hunter, daughter of jazz great Slim Gailliard, and in a flipped situation from his marriage with Anna, she was 17 years Gaye's junior. At the time, he was 34 and she was barely 17, but they still moved in together and would eventually have two children, Nona Marvisa Gaye and Frankie Christian Gaye, before Gaye was officially divorced from Anna. It is thought that Hunter was the inspiration for much of Gaye's next large-scale project, *Let's Get It On*, as sexualized an album as *What's Going On* had been political.

By the early '70s, a lot more than Gaye's subject matter and social emergence was changing at Motown. The studio tried to develop additional vocal abilities by having Gaye develop a "tough man"[225] side to his sweet singing voice, a request that came in the form of a command where Norman Whitfield's songs were concerned. Whitfield preferred a "sharper raspy voice,"[226] but understandably, Gaye was not thrilled at the prospect and was not a fan of the Whitfield songs, most of which "he profusely disliked."[227] Nonetheless, by the time Gaye's vocal transformation was finished, he had three useable vocal personas: "his smooth, sweet tenor, a growling rasp, and an unreal falsetto."[228] One observer reported that when he used all three on separate tracks that were subsequently mixed, it resembled "the ancient art of weaving."[229]

Also in 1971, Gaye was slated to record a series of duets with Diana Ross, including a remake of one he had sung with Tammi Terrell. By now, Gaye was accustomed to smoking marijuana at will in the studio, so when Ross, who was carrying her first child, requested that he forego the habit for one session, he refused. As a result, Ross recorded her tracks in a separate studio.

No more albums emerged until 1972, the year that a Marvin Gaye Day was announced in Washington, D.C., complete with a key to the city. For the most part, the year was spent

---

[223] FAM People.com, Marvin Gaye Biography – www.fampeople.com/cat-marvin-gaye_6
[224] FAM People.com
[225] FAM People.com
[226] FAM People.com
[227] FAM People.com
[228] FAM People.com
[229] FAM People.com

recording the next major hit, *Let's Get It On*, a sexually explicit collection that has been called "one of the most revered anthems of all time,"[230] and the second of his efforts to reach number 1 on Billboard. During this time, Motown pushed Gaye into touring, and he reluctantly obeyed by collaborating with Diana Ross and the Miracles. In another detour made possible by his varied talents, he took the time to do a score for the thriller film *Trouble Man*, and the title track notched another top 10 for Gaye. *Trouble Man* was intended as a soundtrack for what is commonly called a "blaxpoitation film," centered around the character of Mr. T, and the album reached the top twenty in Billboard, peaking at number 12. Gaye was awarded the Trendsetter Award from Billboard in '72.

Let's Get It On, released in August 1973 as the 12th studio album by Gaye, has gone down in the entire music industry's history as "one of the most sexually charged albums ever recorded."[231] In fact, some of the tracks were withheld from promotion due to their graphic nature, such as "You Sure Love to Ball." The title track and "Come Get to This" are nearly as controversial, comprising an album that is "unparalleled in its sheer sensuality and carnal energy."[232] The album took the better part of three years to record, the result of touring and non-professional considerations; Gaye would spend much of the early '70s attempting to deal with his crumbling marriage to Anna, with whom he was still professionally intertwined.

The solo effort, *I Want You*, was delayed, and in 1973, Gaye teamed again with Diana Ross for a duet collection entitled *Marvin and Diana*. The release was not immediately forthcoming, and once issued, it was heavily criticized for lacking the sense of intimacy that Gaye had achieved with Tammi Terrell. To cover up the general gap in Gaye's output, Motown released a concert recorded live in England, *Live at the London Palladium*, and he had just one release of a single for the year.

In September 1974, Hunter gave birth to their daughter, Nona Marvisa Gaye, and in November of the following year, she gave birth to their son Frankie. Meanwhile, Anna Gordy Gaye, after the long-term conflict between the two, filed for divorce, but a lengthy and bitter fight would be waged over the coming year, point by point. Anna claimed to be owed an enormous sum in withheld royalty payments as part of the settlement, and the court agreed, ordering Gaye to pay all missed alimony and to record a new album from which all the proceeds would go to back payments. The "settlement negotiations were brutal,"[233] and the figure of contention, legally certified by 1976, was said to amount to over a $500,000. Despite running out of money, Gaye was honored that year by the United Nations for his charitable work.

While that was going on, Gaye was already working on the album *I Want You*, an effort that was called by one critic "a suite of overwhelming libidinous energy."[234] The new album was an

[230] Bio.com, Marvin Gaye
[231] Jason Ankeny, all Music
[232] Guide Chart.com, Marvin Gaye – www.guidechart.com/marvin-gaye-biography.php
[233] David Ritz, Marvin Gaye Biography

attempt at writing something akin to disco, a genre that did not particularly interest Gaye, and in a sense, the project spoke to his morbid "shyness and obsessional fear of dancing."[235] Gaye had, as usual, resisted, explaining that "Motown was screaming disco at me, but I couldn't be bothered."[236]

The divorce process dragged on through 1977, and Gaye was still saddled with the "alimony album." He began the project with no enthusiasm whatsoever, but as time went on, it became a tool for venting his long-held frustration. By the time he completed *Here, My Dear*, he had created a scathing double album that described the intimate woes of his marriage to Anna in detail. Ironically, it would be the last of its kind released by Motown, with Gordy bearing the dilemma of promoting an album that savaged his sister but also paid her what she was due.

A bitter commentary from first to last, the album was released in December 1978 after it had been recorded over the past year in Gaye's personal studio in Los Angeles. At first, the album was both a commercial and critical disaster, but through the years following Gaye's death, critics have begun to hail it as an example of his high quality work. Difficult as it was to put his heart into an album for which he would receive no payment, not to mention other obviously ironic elements, Gaye actually grew intrigued with the idea, and by his own description, "I sang and sang until I drained everything I'd lived through."[237] It seems he had decided that even for this project, listeners deserved his best.

Motown withheld the release of *Here, My Dear* for a year, and during that time, Gaye worked on another sizeable project entitled *Lover Man*, but it was rejected by the studio and scrapped entirely when the single "Ego Trippin' Out" failed to reach the charts. Gaye had finally been cleared to marry Hunter, which he did, but by this time, that marriage was failing as well. When Gaye was divorced from Janis Hunter by 1979, she and the children moved to the home of her mother, and Marvin moved in with his.

Beginning a subsequent tour strung out and exhausted, Gaye landed without the makings of a real plan in Hawaii. After a career's worth of conflict, Gaye's relationship with Gordy and Motown came to an end as well after the record company released *In Our Lifetime*. Gaye thought it was entirely unfit for publication, especially since it was completed without his consultation or permission. Furthermore, it was Gaye's contention that the studio mangled it along the way, both in terms of music and artwork; he claimed that the label remixed and edited the album without contacting him on any occasion, altered the title of the album by removing the intended question mark, and supplied the cover with artwork that was a poor parody of his own. Gaye charged Motown with releasing "an essentially unfinished album without his permission,"[238] one that he

[234] David Ritz, Marvin Gaye Biography

[235] David Ritz, Marvin Gaye Biography

[236] David Ritz, PBS American Masters

[237] PBS, American Masters, Marvin Gaye Timeline – www.pbs.org/wnet/americanmasters/episodes/marvin-gaye/career-timeline/74/

[238] Encyclopedia.com, Marvin Gaye

had intended to refine as the most philosophical of his works to that point, a loftier foil to the two previous releases that were slanted toward disco. Given what he believed to be a serious injustice done against him, and the mood already created due to his failed marriage with Anna, there was nothing more to be done. As a result, Gaye severed his relationship forever with Motown after two long and fruitful (if not altogether satisfying), decades. As Gaye once put it succinctly, "Detroit turned out to be heaven, but it also turned out to be hell."

Chapter 6: Final Years

"I sing about life." – Marvin Gaye

In Our Lifetime, without the question mark, was in the stores by 1981 after a year of recording, and Gaye was released from his contract when Columbia Records bought out the remainder. In debt to the IRS for over $4.5 million, he had also "jumped ship" in Hawaii, causing colleagues no end of inconvenience, and was living in a bread van, destitute and searching for cocaine money wherever he could find it. It has even been purported that he called his mother on one occasion and asked her to sell her jewelry.

Gaye's next project was already in the works as he relocated to Europe under even greater pressure from the IRS. Offered a place in Ostend, Belgium, he met with David Ritz to collaborate on "Sexual Healing," which would be released in September 1982. The single, which would be part of the upcoming album *Midnight Love*, would go on to win two Grammys, one for Favorite Soul Single, and an American Music Award. Gaye performed the famous song at the Grammy Awards in a silk robe and bikini underwear, evoking a mixed fan reaction.

As that performance demonstrated, Gaye was beginning to get a reputation aside from his music, and he was noteworthy as much for his personal troubles as he was for his records. Stories of erratic behavior abounded as "humor and easy charm gave way to paranoia and fear,"[239] and what was to be a big comeback under the auspices of Columbia was hampered by Gaye's increasing cocaine addiction and mental instability. On one hand, he threatened to quit and become a monk, but on a moment's notice, he would then rant and rave about being a bigger sex symbol than Elvis Presley.

Regardless, for the musical basis of "Sexual Healing," Gaye had settled on a rhythm track somewhat outside of the norm, "a reggae-style rhythm track from keyboardist Odell Brown that he was obsessed with…he knew that the track had potential."[240] Gaye and Ritz had been friends for years, and the author joined him in Ostend for the specific purpose of working on the song and accompanying tracks for the album. Among the first things Ritz encountered was a large avant-garde book on Gaye's coffee table that was filled with page after page of sexual brutality.

---

[239] David Ritz, Marvin Gaye Biography
[240] Songwriter Universe, "Amazing Saga; the detailed story of how author David Ritz wrote Sexual Healing with Marvin Gaye – www.songwriteruniverse.com/davidritz.html

As Ritz recalls it, he said to Gaye, "This is sick – what you need is sexual healing."[241] Gaye immediately asked if Ritz would write the lyrics, and despite his inexperience with that genre of writing, he agreed, eventually supplying the bulk of the lyrics heard in the final result.

According to Ritz, Gaye was experiencing some relief from his anxiety in Belgium, and despite the cocaine use, he probably should have stayed longer. Describing him as "healthier and more psychologically stable living in the peaceful setting of Belgium,"[242] Gaye's premature return to the United States caused him to enter an "emotional free fall."[243] Ritz, who would eventually file a law suit against Gaye for not affording him credit as a writer on "Sexual Healing," would later observe that in his opinion, "Marvin never got the healing he sang about in the song. He sang it beautifully, but he couldn't quite live up to the message."[244]

Despite their problems, more than one reviewer of Ritz's biography has complained about the way Ritz portrayed Gaye. According to reviewer Charles Keil, who met with Ritz (an atypical event for a biography's review), issue must be taken with the claim that "Let's Get It On" developed from a purely religious urge in which Gaye was striving to "get out of the pain of the present, and next to an all-problem-solving God." Behind the façade of religious angst, he believes that Ritz links suffering to creativity as a requirement for all work that is unique and powerful, and that Gaye's "body of suffering" equates to his "body of work." To Keil, this is absurd, and he seems to assert that to suffer is not a necessary part of artistic work quality, that none of the self-inflicted tragedies in Gaye's life had to happen, and that without the extra drama, Gaye would have gotten more done. Ultimately, Keil decried "Ritz' insistence that Marvin Gaye was a great, individual, creative, suffering, artist, when all the details reveal a good-looking, expert singer totally dependent on the collaboration of composers, producers, musicians, drug dealers, hookers, wives, friends, the astrological tables, etc."[245] Anna Mazama, in reviewing Michael Eric Dyson's prominent biography of Gaye, takes similar exception to Dyson's "troubling assumption that sexuality is key to understanding the artist. Even childhood beatings speak of 'the sexualized brutality of the whippings'…our reliance on sexuality becomes quite annoying at times, [and leaves us] open to wild, cheap speculation."[246]

Gaye cut a tour of Europe short by failing to appear on time at the Royal Gala Charity Show, leaving his British audience greatly offended, and in 1983, Gaye returned to the U.S. following a brief affair with Lady Edith Foxwell, ex-wife of film director Ivan Foxwell. It's been claimed that Gaye and Edith had reportedly discussed marriage before his untimely death.

---

[241] David Ritz, Marvin Gaye Biography

[242] Songwriter Universe

[243] Songwriter Universe

[244] Songwriter Universe

[245] Keil, Charles, Review of David Ritz, "Divided Soul: The Life of Marvin Gaye", in The Society for Ethnomusicology Vol. 31 No. 2, 1987, p. 369

[246] Anna Mazama, Review of Michael Eric Dyson's "Mercy Mercy Me, the Art, Loves and Demons of Marvin Gaye", in African American Review Vol. 40 No. 2, Summer 2006

Upon his return, Gaye was able to make peace, of a sort, with Berry Gordy on a TV special honoring Motown. Also in 1983, he was noted for singing what has been called a "soulful and idiosyncratic" rendition of the national anthem at an NBA All-Star game. This performance, which others called "bizarre" and "absurd," would be Gaye's final performance before the public.

Gaye may have thought that he had nowhere else to go, but his decision to return home and live with his parents in Los Angeles was ill-fated. The steady regimen of violent fights with his father was as it had always been, and as his musical inspirations wound down, Gaye remarked that he "no longer made music for pleasure...I record so that I can feed people what they need, what they feel. Hopefully, I record so that I can help someone overcome a bad time."[247]

Gaye and Gordon Banks in February 1984

Gaye's debt to the IRS had become astronomical by 1984, and his assets were seized wherever possible, including his recording studio in Los Angeles. Unable to maintain a steady relationship and living in the childhood environment of his father's anger, he turned more inward and became

---

[247] Bio.com, Marvin Gaye Biography

even more addicted and controlled by paranoia. Convinced that he was being stalked by assassins of an unknown origin, Gaye began to take an interest in weaponry, stockpiled guns throughout the house, and wore a bulletproof vest on a regular basis, even while he slept. He kept a pistol in his robe and "had a small arsenal under his bed,"[248] including a cheap machine gun that he only got rid of after much pleading from his mother. During the sparse work he was able to get done in the studio (his cocaine use making serious work all but impossible), Gaye was constantly surrounded by a bevy of bodyguards. He recorded armed and in a vest as well.

Among the weapons Gaye collected was an unregistered Smith & Wesson 38 caliber handgun which he presented to his father for Christmas 1984, an odd choice of gift considering their "long-festering, pathological relationship."[249] On April 1, 1984, the decision proved to be lethal in the wake of an argument between Gay, Sr. and Alberta over the whereabouts of some insurance documents. An agitated Gaye attempted to intervene on his mother's behalf, and the typical shouting match ensued. Gaye forced his father out of an upstairs room and out into the hallway, knocking him down and allegedly kicking him. The older man retired to his room, re-emerged with the Smith & Wesson, and "shot him in the chest"[250] before firing again. The first bullet perforated Gaye's right lung, heart, diaphragm, liver, stomach, and left kidney, and was deemed to be "immediately fatal,"[251] although others have said that he was able to speak a few words to his brother, who had come running at the shots. Gaye allegedly said, "I got what I wanted...I couldn't do it myself, so I made him do it."[252] Such an occurrence seems unlikely, however, as the first shot would have almost certainly incapacitated speech, not to mention the fact that Gay, Sr. "stepped forward and fired again at point blank range...[then] went downstairs and threw the pistol on the lawn, sat and waited for the police."[253] It was Frankie Gay's wife, Irene, who called in the shooting.

According to David Krajicek of Crime Library, Gaye's death "reads like a Biblical parable – man hollers at wife, son defending mother hollers back at father. Father hollers at son. Son smites father, father kills son."[254] One might also surmise from the lifelong bitterness between the two men that something of this nature might eventually occur, but even for the two combatants, "their venomous antipathy was deeper than either man had understood."[255]

Gaye was rushed to California Medical Center, where he was pronounced dead at 1:01 pm, and his father was subsequently arrested and taken in. Asked in a preliminary interview whether Gay, Sr. loved his son, he is said to have answered, "Let's say that I didn't dislike him,"[256] and he

[248] Find a Death.com, Marvin Gaye – www.findadeath.com/Deceased/9/MarvinGaye/marvin_gaye.htm
[249] David Krajicek, Crime Library
[250] IMDb, Marvin Gaye Biography
[251] Find a Death.com
[252] This Day in History
[253] Find a Death.com
[254] David Krajicek, Crime Library
[255] David Ritz, Marvin Gaye Biography
[256] Find a Death.com

repeated his claims that he had acted in self-defense. His case was not without some merit, as at the time of arrest, his body bore visible bruises, apparently at the hands of his son. Before the end of trial, for which he was judged competent, Gay, Sr. was also found to have a brain tumor, and eventually received a six-year suspended sentence after accepting a "no contest" plea for voluntary manslaughter.

Following the second family shooting of her life, Alberta Cooper Gay sued for divorce and moved in with her daughter. Three years later, she would die of bone cancer in Los Angeles. Her son had been killed one day before his 45th birthday, and he was planning to work with Barry White the following week in an attempt to revive his professional life. In 1998, Marvin Gay, Sr. died of pneumonia at the age of 84 in a nursing home

The public had experienced and would continue to experience the untimely deaths of numerous musical celebrities, many shocking in their own right, from Buddy Holly's fatal plane crash to the murder of John Lennon, but "few deaths in the annals of American pop music stand out as more bewildering, senseless and tragic…the man who chased away the demons of millions…was chased by demons of his own throughout his life."[257] Marvin Gaye was given a "star-studded funeral"[258] after lying in state at Forest Lawn in an open-casket service. It is estimated that over 10,000 mourners attended, including his mother, Anna Gordy, Janis Hunter, and his three children. During the service, Smokey Robinson and Stevie Wonder offered "heartfelt eulogies,"[259] after which Gaye's remains were cremated and his ashes were scattered over the Pacific Ocean.

Chapter 7: Marvin Gaye's Legacy

In 1985, Columbia Records issued two collections of Gaye's music, most of them outtakes, entitled *Dream of a Lifetime*, a collection that one critic called "a compilation of erotic funk workouts"[260] alongside romantic and spiritual ballads. A second compilation released in the same year was entitled *Romantically Yours*, a collection that has been described as a "vulnerable" collection of ballads that took over 12 years to complete. It is difficult to determine whether Gaye would have approved the release of *Dream of a Lifetime* given that many of the tracks included were "seconds," such as takes of "Savage in the Sack" and "Masochistic Beauty."

Tributes to Gaye started to pour in almost immediately after his death. The Spandau Ballet choreographed his single "True" after the shooting, and The Commodores referenced him in the 1985 song "Nightshift." Diana Ross released "Missing You," and an album track recorded by Teena Marie was titled "My Dear Mr. Gaye."

Gaye was inducted into the Rock & Roll Hall of Fame in 1987, and two years later, Frankie

---

[257] Top Documentary Films – "Marvin Gaye: His Final Hours" – www.topdocumentaryfilms.com/marvin-gaye-his-final-hours/
[258] Rock & Roll Hall of Fame
[259] Encyclopedia.com, Marvin Gaye
[260] Jason Ankeny, All Music

Beverly honored him with *Silky Soul*. Eddie Murphy took a leading role in honoring Gaye at the installation of his Walk of Fame Star. Israeli artist Izahr Asdot dedicated a song to Gaye entitled "Eesh Hashokolad" (Chocolate Man) in 1992, and three years later, Madonna and Gaye's daughter Nona sang together in an MTV-produced album called *Inner City Blues: The Music of Marvin Gaye*. The tributes continued with offerings from such artists as Brian McKnight, Christina Aguilera, Bono, Mariah Carey, The Backstreet Boys, Britney Spears, and numerous others.

In 2008, *Rolling Stone* ranked Gaye at number 6 among the Greatest Singers of All Times, a high honor considering the vast field from which to choose. In the same year, Gaye earned $3.5 million posthumously, placing him at number 13 on Forbes list of "Top Earning Dead Celebrities." In 2013, son Marvin Gaye III required a transplant to deal with kidney failure and underwent a serious regimen of medical procedures, while his first wife, Anna, died at the age of 92 in 2014.

As with other musical luminaries who die at a young age, people cannot help but wonder what works might have come out in Gaye's subsequent years. There is no reason to believe that Marvin Gaye would have stayed in a traditional regimen for long, because he clearly "loved to shock" and "relished surprise."[261] Gaye gave listeners an ample share of innovation through the twists and turns of his musical evolution, and each of his major artistic components received a turn at expression through his years at Motown. Those who listened to all his albums got a chance to hear his beautiful singing voice, his flair for dance music, his frustration and rage over his troubled childhood, his raw sexuality as an object of adoration, his social philosophies, and his righteousness indignation at disturbing social issues. He brought his instrumental skills to numerous artists in the early years and his production skills to his own later works, changing the way even the stiffly-run Motown did business. At the end of it all, however, spanning personal heartbreak and professional disappointment, one central pursuit remained: the urge to explore. As he put it, "I hope to refine music, study it, try to find some area that I can unlock…these can't be the only notes in the world, there's got to be other notes someplace, in some dimension, between the cracks on the piano keys."[262]

The 1960s were unquestionably a producer-driven decade, but "Gaye changed all that."[263] Starting out by pursuing a track quite different than the one to which the fates eventually took him, Gaye, with his unusually attractive tenor voice, succeeded in almost every genre he touched, and he eventually "outgrew the crowd-pleasing sound that made Motown famous."[264] Indeed, Gaye reached such a state of acclaim that even Berry Gordy, founder and Chief

[261] David Ritz, Marvin Gaye Biography

[262] David Ritz, Marvin Gaye Biography

[263] David Ritz, PBS American Masters, Marvin Gaye, "What's Going On – PBS.org/wnet/americanmasters/episodes/marvin-gaye/whats-going-on/73

[264] This Day in History, Marvin Gaye's shot and killed by his own father – www.history.com/this-day-in-history/marvin-gaye-is-shot-and-killed-by-his-father

Executive of the iconic Motown, was left with no choice but to allow him a wider degree of artistic control.

Gaye has been described by historians, critics, and colleagues as "a self-taught singer with a flair for autobiographical revelation,"[265] a charming and sweet colleague with "a quick wit…a natural storyteller."[266] However, as the autocratic Gordy would later learn, when it came to a test of wills, Gaye could defend his top priorities at extreme levels, bringing a host of accumulated personal qualities he had honed in a terrifying and humiliating childhood. His soft-spoken nature was not to be taken for granted, for Gaye was many things to many situations, "an anti-authoritarian artist – shy, ambitious, mellow, but fearful, brooding and serious."[267] At the same time, those who grew frustrated with Gaye's obstinate nature knew that he was also "one of the most gifted, visionary and enduring talents"[268] ever to come through Motown. Taking on the moniker "Prince of Soul," he rose from a childhood of church singing to work as a session man for well-known artists, excelling in the realm of sensual and romantic ballads before eventually joining the protest genre in the Vietnam era. He even gave a late career tip of the hat to disco, however much he disliked pandering to trendy dance music trends. Although it was in the genres of soul and R&B, two forms melded by their own evolution, that Gaye "monumentally influenced,"[269] and in which he would become a giant, it became apparent that his natural gifts and instincts could have succeeded almost anywhere. Creating some of the best-crafted songs of the '60s and selling records at a furious rate, Marvin Gaye took "lean, powerful R&B to stylish, sophisticated soul…[and then] finally [to] an entirely political and personal form of artistic expression. One of Motown's Renaissance men, Gaye could do it all."[270]

When it came to Gaye the musician, even those who despaired over the self-destructive path of his personal life could not diminish him in terms of pure talent. His chief biographer, David Ritz, who not only interviewed Gaye but became friends with him and co-wrote the lyrics to one of his most revered songs, describes the music as "cathartic. His songs were prayers, meditations, strategies for survival."[271] Gaye's initial reaction to many of the song texts presented to him seemed unenthused, but in almost every case, he found what was needed to give an "inspired reading."[272]

Marvin Gaye was not primarily a stage performer, although he undertook his fair share of media and touring performances. As a live singer, he was prone to excessive nervousness, so he could go for extensive periods of time without poking his head out of the recording studio, which

---

[265] David Ritz, PBS American Masters
[266] David Ritz, PBS American Masters
[267] David Ritz, PBS American Masters
[268] Jason Ankeny, All Music.com, Artist Blog, Marvin Gaye – www.allmusic.com/artist/marvin-gaye-mn0000316834/biography
[269] Jason Ankeny, All Music.com
[270] Rock & Roll Hall of Fame, Marvin Gaye Biography – www.rockhall.com/inductees/marvin-gaye/bio
[271] Rock & Roll Hall of Fame
[272] Rolling Stone Artists, Marvin Gaye Biography – www.rollingstone.com/music/artists/marvin-gaye/biography

was his true artistic home. He avoided television whenever possible, and he often did not appear as scheduled when he agreed to perform live. Minimally reliable on many fronts, he was, however, rock solid before the studio microphone, "one of the most consistent and [albeit] enigmatic of the Motown hitmakers."[273]

The original aspirations of this well-traveled artist began in another area entirely, and the early conflicts in his life were not so much about which genre to choose, but about how to avoid the dangers of an upbringing in which no secular music of any kind was allowed in the home. The degree of rebellion to which Gaye was pushed as a young man included the fantasy of becoming a club singer in the mold of a black Frank Sinatra. He admired the suave, romantic ballad above all other styles, and it seemed a natural choice given his "mellifluous tenor"[274] voice. Similarly inspired by Nat King Cole, Ray Charles, and Perry Como, his appearance on the Motown scene came with the assumption that this would be his path. Only after several attempts, with which neither the studio nor Gaye was satisfied, did they begin to consider the later course of "quiet storm, urban contemporary, slow-jam, and soul music."[275]

In reshaping Gaye's musical and public image following his early releases, Motown did not abandon his qualities of suave and alluring intimacy. The studio struck gold by pairing the good-looking Gaye with several of their greatest female artists, and his fame as a duet singer still stands unchallenged. The first experiment was with Mary Wells, followed by Kim West and the legendary Diana Ross. The most successful relationship, however, emerged from his pairing with Tammi Terrell, and their iconic duets together "are the standard against which all R&B duos are measured."[276]

As the external world left the themes of village love and simple stories of attraction behind for immediate and pressing world issues, Motown dug in its heels and refused to let Gaye leave the safe confines of traditional topics. However, after he had provided the record company with a string of unparalleled successes, he did the unthinkable by refusing to sing another note until his wish to assume greater control over his career was accommodated. Following a lengthy stalemate, the single for "What's Going On" was released as nothing more than an act of appeasement, only to become one of the most revered examples of protest in an already rich field of songwriters and performers. By transforming "predominantly soulful R&B to more socially conscious lyrics reflective of the tenor of the late 60s and 70s,"[277] Marvin Gaye joined the modern world as a musical and social spokesman, and to a great degree, he managed to bring the rigid Motown with him.

---

[273] Rolling Stone Artists
[274] Rolling Stone Artists
[275] R&B Hall of Fame, Marvin Gaye – www.rbhalloffame.com/marvin-gaye/
[276] David Ritz. PBS American Masters
[277] NPR Music, What's Going On: A Departure That Defined a Generation – www.npr.org/2011/06/01/136818199/whats-going-on-defined-a-generation

Florence Lefranc's painting of Gaye

Aretha Franklin

Chapter 1: Growing Up in Washington, D.C.

"Being a singer is a natural gift. It means I'm using to the highest degree possible the gift that God gave me to use. I'm happy with that." – Aretha Franklin

Aretha Franklin was born in Memphis, Tennessee, on March 25, 1942. Her parents, both of whom would play crucial roles in shaping her identity and choice in career, were Barbara and Clarence (known as C.L. to everyone). She had five siblings, including three sisters (Erma, Carolyn, and Carl) and two brothers (Vaughan and Cecil), although two of them were from her parents' previous marriages (or relationships). Memphis would prove to be a city to which Aretha would have little connection, as the family made the rather unlikely move to Buffalo, New York when Aretha was just two years of age, as C.L. found work there as a preacher. As it happened, Aretha's time in upstate New York would prove to be nearly as short-lived as her early years in Memphis.

Thomas R Machnitzki's picture of Aretha's birthplace in Memphis

It is worth noting that Aretha's parents were not particularly young by the time Aretha was born, particularly when one takes into consideration the social conventions of the time period. C.L. was 27 years old (although his age has been contested, with some reporting that he may have been several years younger), while Barbara was two years younger (Ritz). More significantly, they had each suffered unsuccessful marriages, and their own marriage would suffer as well. Barbara was born and raised in Shelby, Mississippi. Her first child, Vaughn, was the product of an early relationship, and the father (to whom Barbara was not married) was not involved in the parenting process. Not long after giving birth to Vaughn, Barbara met C.L., and C.L. became the legal father of Vaughan. C.L. and Barbara married on June 3, 1936, and began raising a family not long thereafter. Their first child together, Erma, was born in 1938, followed by Cecil (1940), Aretha (1942), and Carolyn (1944).

It does not take wild speculation to see why C.L. and Barbara were attracted to each other, as they were each musically inclined. For her part, Barbara was an excellent pianist and also a talented vocalist. Meanwhile, C.L. possessed one of the finest gospel singing voices in the nation, and this gift would catapult him to national celebrity during Aretha's upbringing. Barbara and C.L. were also quite attractive, although it would be from Barbara that Aretha would inherit the majority of her physical characteristics, notably her soft eyes. Although neither Barbara nor her husband had any lingering connection to Memphis, preaching provided C.L. and his wife with the opportunity for upward mobility. The son of a sharecropper, C.L. had experienced extreme poverty while growing up in the Deep South, and even before he became famous, he was able to comfortably provide for Aretha and her siblings through his employment as pastor.

One of the deep ironies of C.L. Franklin is that as fervent as he was in his devotion to the church, he was incapable of remaining with just one woman, a fact that would eventually compromise his marriage beyond repair. During Aretha's earliest years, Barbara tolerated his infidelities, but the marriage was never particularly close as a result of his philandering. In the words of Aretha's brother, Cecil, "His loyalty was essentially to God, his children, and his congregation. He was never going to be a one-woman man. In contrast, Mother was certainly a one-man woman" (Ritz). Just before Aretha turned five years of age, the family moved from Buffalo to Detroit, where C.L. was hired to serve as pastor for the newly-established New Bethel Baptist Church. This proved to be an enormously-consequential move, not only because it gave C.L. a new audience and location, but also (this would become significant years later, during Aretha's adolescence) because Detroit became an epicenter for gospel-influenced rock music— the genre known as "Motown." From a business standpoint at least, moving to Detroit was undoubtedly one of the wisest decisions that C.L. ever made.

However, Barbara was not content in Detroit and became unable to live with her husband's womanizing. Just one year after moving to Detroit, Barbara took her first son, Vaughn, and moved back to Buffalo. This was a turning point in Aretha's life, although the exact effect it had on Aretha remains one of the greatest points of contestation among Aretha's biographers. To be certain, separating from her mother caused significant anguish, the effects of which were exacerbated due to the fact that Barbara's departure occurred virtually without warning. Aretha had always been particularly close to her mother, and Craig Werner notes in his study of Aretha, "Many of those who knew Aretha well believe that Barbara's departure and death affected Aretha even more deeply than she acknowledged". For her part, however, Aretha would always be quick to downplay the anxieties resulting from the departure of her mother.

In the end, the life of Aretha's mother stands as one of the most tragic aspects of Aretha Franklin's life. Not only was she unhappy in marriage, but she would pass away abruptly on March 7, 1952, the victim of a heart attack. Aretha would always speak fondly of her mother, and she shared her mother's soft disposition (in contrast with C.L.'s loud—literally and figuratively—presence). Even without the presence of her mother, it was not as if Aretha was bereft of female authority figures in her life, as C.L. began a serious relationship with another woman not long after Barbara's departure. There was also a bevy of woman who would assist in the child-rearing tasks, including her grandmother, Rachel. In fact, it was from her grandmother that Aretha learned how to play piano by ear. However, the death of her mother was a hurdle that was particularly difficult to overcome.

With C.L. as the domineering father of the household, it was rather inevitable that the Franklin household was defined by religion and gospel music, with the two going hand-in-hand in C.L.'s preaching. Education was a distant priority compared to the church, and C.L. encouraged each of his children to develop their singing talents. It was clear from the outset that Aretha possessed a singular gift, inheriting her father's powerful voice. Because she never recorded any performances from these early years, we do not possess any extant records of her singing from these childhood years. However, Franklin grew up in the company of a veritable roster of Motown greats, one of whom was Smokey Robinson, who later characterized Aretha thusly: "[A]ll I could do was view Aretha as a wonder child. Mind you, this was Detroit, where musical talent ran strong and free. Everyone was singing and harmonizing; everyone was playing piano and guitar. Aretha came out of this world, but she also came out of another far-off magical world none of us really understood. She came from a distant musical planet where children are born with their gifts fully formed." (Ritz)

Smokey Robinson and The Miracles

Robinson's description makes evident Aretha's innate talent, and the extent to which her voice carried the legacy of her father. Even compared to the talented Motown singers in whose company she grew up, Franklin's voice was distinctive. She received vocal training to be sure, but her primary challenge would not involve mastering the fundamentals of singing but rather mastering the art of performing before an audience.

Aretha was educated in local schools throughout her elementary school years, but by high school it was clear that the profession she would eventually work in would involve the church, singing, or (in the spirit of her father) some combination therein. Of course, it is entirely possible that, had she been raised in a household that privileged the classroom education experience, Aretha may have been more inclined to continue with her studies. However, C.L. had been raised during a period in which the educated African- American was just emerging as a social construct. In these debates, two camps formed: on the one hand, those who followed W.E.B. Du Bois in arguing that blacks needed to receive a college education; and on the other, those who adopted Booker T. Washington's position that a technical education was optimal (Ritz). C.L. subscribed to the Washington camp and emphasized the pragmatism of a more skill-oriented education over the more humanistic classroom model. With this in mind, before entering high school, Aretha ended her studies and effectively began her music career.

Chapter 2: The Gospel Circuit

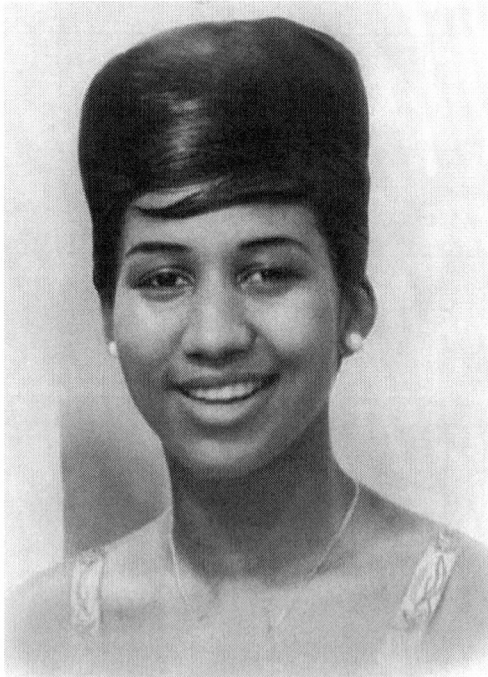

Young Aretha Franklin

"Let's start with the church. As you know, it's my background, it's a natural setting for me and it's definitely my roots." – Aretha Franklin

When Aretha Franklin ended her studies to focus exclusively on her performing career, this was not actually the beginning of her role as a musical performer, as she had started singing before an audience several years earlier, before the death of her mother. It is believed, in fact, that her first song was the hymn "Jesus, Be a Fence Around Me" (McAvoy). One of the great benefits of having C.L. as her father was that she was never wanting for opportunities to perform in public, and indeed the majority of her earliest performances were at the New Bethel Church. By the time Aretha reached her teenage years, C.L. had developed an electric, almost cult-like following at New Bethel, an achievement that was perhaps due more to his abilities as a singer than his virtues as an actual preacher. To this end, singer Bobby "Blue" Bland would later describe C.L. with this glowing characterization: "I liked church 'cause of the exciting spirit of the music, but when the preachers got to preaching, I'd get bored and fidgety. But here comes this man with this voice like a singer. In fact, he did sing before he started into preaching—and that got my attention right off. Can't tell you what hymn he sang, but his voice was strong. I sat right up and my mind didn't wander anywhere. He grabbed my attention and kept it." (Ritz)

Bobby "Blue" Bland

This description speaks to the way in which C.L.'s success as a preacher stemmed largely from the singularity of his voice, but there is also a way in which his voice held a melodic quality, even while not technically singing. C.L. Franklin benefitted greatly from his historical moment, specifically through the advancements in electronic technology. His vocal talents were formidable enough to earn him a syndicated radio program, which broadened his exposure. Concurrent with these broadcasts, he began getting hired to travel around the country giving sermons, earning thousands of dollars in the process (Dobkin). These performances both live and on radio, catapulted him into something of a celebrity and a major figure in the black community. His radio broadcasts not only included his sermons but also involved gospel music performances and commentary on current events; in other words, he held a fairly prominent platform through. Here it is also worth noting that the Franklins first arrived in Detroit just three years prior to the outbreak of the race riots in the city. As a celebrity, it was inevitable that C.L. would become acquainted with many of the most significant names in the black community, and he would become close to both Martin Luther King, Jr. and Jesse Jackson. C.L. Franklin's name is not often invoked in discussion of the Civil Rights Movement, but if one applies a more granular look at Detroit specifically, one can see that Franklin was a key figure who galvanized the black community even beyond the confines of the New Bethel Church.

The majority of C.L.'s travels were through what is colloquially referred to as his "gospel caravan" tours. It should be noted that his primary responsibility in these performances was not specifically to sing, but rather to preach (which was accompanied by singing). As noted earlier, the genius of C.L. Franklin was that he was able to preach in an almost musical manner, thereby bridging the traditionally firm distinction in the church service between the singing of gospel hymns and the more restrained formal prayer. When Aretha accompanied her father, her task, on the other hand, revolved exclusively around singing. This singing, it should also be noted, was exclusively gospel-related, standing in mild contrast with her later music, which incorporated pronounced elements of rock. Put differently, with these early-career performances, Aretha performed for what was a more hermetic, exclusively-religious public. While her audience paled in comparison with the public she was able to reach with her chart-topping hits later in her career, she gained valuable performing experience, experience that was particularly useful for someone as shy as Aretha was during her teenage years.

The gospel circuit that C.L. partook in has few modern equivalents, although there were cross-cultural parallels in other racial and ethnic traditions in the United States. Chief among these was the vaudeville comedy circuit, particularly that of Jewish vaudeville. Leading up until around 1925, vaudeville had served as one of America's premier entertainment mediums, with troupes of vaudeville players traveling the country to perform their routines, most of which involved comedy, but some of which also contained more dramatic musical performances. The cultural phenomenon of a traveling performer who is tasked with playing in front of a new audience in a new setting from week to week derived (in America, at least) largely from vaudeville. In this respect, it is no accident that one of C.L.'s performing idols was Al Jolson. Today, Jolson is remembered for his landmark performance in the movie *The Jazz Singer*, the first feature film to implement synchronized sound. However, before beginning his film career, he had performed on the vaudeville circuit, and it was from this early performing history that he first became a celebrity. While the gospel circuits are often forgotten in discussions of entertainment practice (perhaps because they challenge the line between entertainment on the one hand and a religious Puritanism on the other), it is most accurate to see C.L. Franklin's gospel tours as a kind of African-American equivalent to the famous vaudeville circuits (which had, admittedly, become almost extinct by the time Aretha began performing).

Jolson

If the notion of "gospel tours" might appear at first glance to connote a kind of puritanical cultism, in practice the tours were anything but, and presented a challenging way of life for Aretha, who was still early in her teenage years. It was not by accident that the tours were known for being a "sex circus," and because he never traveled with his romantic partner, C.L. took full opportunity to engage in infidelity. There can be no doubt that C.L.'s position as a religious leader was not disingenuous; he believed strongly in the faith, as reflected by his friendship with Martin Luther King, Jr., for example. However, Franklin was also no evangelical, and one of his overriding contradictions is the way in which he could sing and preach with tremendous religious fervor while operating against these same principles when sleeping with other women.

While Aretha would never share the freewheeling sensibilities of her father, touring on the gospel circuit made it rather easy for her to engage in her first sexual forays. At the age of 14, not long after she began touring, Aretha became pregnant. As one would expect, this was not something that she had planned for, and she would later skirt the subject when it was raised (in a wise move, particularly considering the time period). It would be years later before Aretha became involved in a serious relationship, but the early pregnancy stands as evidence of the way in which joining the gospel tour brought Aretha in contact with a new set of temptations that were not available in the more restrained environment of her Detroit home.

Even though C.L. indulged his own passions with little disregard, his acumen as a businessman constitutes one of the more under-acknowledged aspects of Aretha Franklin's rise to fame. By the time Aretha reached her teenage years, C.L. had become a wealthy man, and he possessed a savvy understanding of how to navigate the business climate of the music industry. In 1956, while Aretha was still just 14 years of age, she signed with J.V.B. Records at the behest of her father and her first album, *Songs of Faith*, followed suit. The album was released before the end of the year and included songs such as "You Go Closer" and "Yield Not to Temptation." In a sense, the album was premature, as it would be another five years before her second one was released. Listening to *Songs of Faith*, it is hard not to get the impression that Aretha's voice was not fully developed, and the songs fit neatly into the gospel genre rather than the more complex negotiation between gospel and rock that takes place in Aretha's more mature hits. It is perhaps best to view this first album as a kind of soft start to Aretha Franklin's career, offering an incomplete glance at the talent that would take over America during the following decade.

Thus, the Aretha Franklin that emerged from *Songs of Faith* did not offer much to foreshadow the singer she would later become, and Aretha still needed to undergo the dramatic shift from soul music to the hybrid soul-rock music that she would perfect. This process was not an easy one, and it was also not one that was undertaken with conscious awareness beforehand. In fact, for the few years following *Songs of Faith*, Franklin remained entrenched within the gospel genre. She would continue traveling on the gospel tour until she was 18—four years in total. Aretha did not remain at her father's side all this time, and traveled intermittently with The Caravans and The Soul Stirrers.

Considering that even at age 18, Aretha was still relatively shy and reserved, it is perhaps surprising that she made the dramatic decision to break away from her father's domain and attempt a career as a pop singer. This decision was motivated in large part because her friend (and possible love interest) Sam Cooke (singer for The Soul Stirrers) had just undergone the shift from gospel to pop. Given his outsized personality and visibility within the gospel landscape, one would have expected C.L. to oppose his daughter's ambition, but he offered his support and took an active role in ensuring that she signed with a reputable record label that would effectively manage her career. Under C.L.'s supervision, Aretha packaged a demo of two songs, the strength of which was enough to earn her a contract with John Hammond and Columbia Records. Columbia also arranged for Franklin to work under the tutelage of choreographer Cholly Atkins.

Sam Cooke

Hammond

Atkins

As it happened, Aretha was torn between signing with Columbia and with RCA (the label with which Sam Cooke had signed), but opted for Columbia at her father's behest. The decision to sign with Columbia was without a doubt the more practical business decision, offering Aretha the kind of platform that she could not have achieved even were she to become one of the most decorated singers in the gospel genre. Aretha would later say in retrospect, "Columbia was a wonderful label for me. Wonderful. The records I made there garnered me an audience. I won a number of polls during the years that I was at Columbia. The Downbeat Jazz Poll. Leonard Feather, who was a huge critic back in the day, different polls that he had. The Playboy poll, a number of polls. So the music was great."

At the same time, it was a controversial move for the daughter of C.L. Franklin to shift into a more secular, musical category, and it was in this sense that she relied on the public support of her father in order to skirt charges that she was being a disobedient daughter. Craig Werner explains that C.L. "helped Aretha weather the initial disapproval of the more staid members of the New Bethel congregation over her move away from traditional gospel". Even with the support of C.L., Aretha's departure from gospel was displeasing for many of the members of her father's church in Detroit, but C.L. helped weather the storm and while much of the music that Aretha recorded over the first half of the decade bore little trace of her gospel roots, the religiously-inflected music would become foundational to her celebrity before the end of the decade.

After signing with Columbia, Franklin experienced success from the outset. Her first single under Columbia, "Today I Sing the Blues," reached the top ten of the Hot Rhythm and Blues Sellers chart. There was every reason to expect that Aretha would have a long and storied partnership with Columbia. After all, the Columbia producer who signed Aretha, John Hammond, was also responsible for signing legendary singer Billie Holiday, a singer with whom Aretha would be compared for the rest of her career. Despite the apparent perfect match between singer and record label, however, Aretha struggled to find momentum with Columbia. In January of 1961, her first album with Columbia, *Aretha*, was released. This album remains memorable for the fact that it contains "Won't Be Long," one of the very finest of Franklin's early songs. However, Aretha failed to achieve the kind of commercial success that Columbia expected, and Dunstan Prial notes, "Despite the high quality of the recordings, *Aretha* didn't sell particularly well. The general consensus handed down over the years by pop-music historians and industry types is that record buyers were confused by the eclectic grouping of songs". Prial speaks with the benefit of hindsight, but his remark corroborates the challenge that Columbia had in packaging Aretha Franklin's music properly; a difficult task given the fact that she could dexterously move between pop and gospel. Ultimately, of course, Aretha's success would derive from her ability to synthesize the two registers, but this would take time and one could argue that it only occurred after Aretha left Columbia.

Aretha's personal life underwent changes that were as significant as those taking place professionally. Where C.L. supported Aretha's move from gospel to pop, however, he was less sanguine about his daughter's romantic decisions. In 1961, still less than 20 years of age, Aretha married for the first time. In fact, the marriage blurred the line between the personal and private in its own way, as her spouse, Ted White, was also her business manager. Given his profession, it is not hard to see why C.L. disapproved of his daughter's choice in spouse. Since Aretha had begun performing, C.L. had effectively operated as her manager, and done so with a remarkable degree of success (considering that he had no business training). In marrying her manager, Aretha was not only distancing herself from having C.L. as her manager but also welcoming her manager into her life in the most intimate level possible.

As it happened, C.L. was justified in his dislike for Ted White, as the marriage was fraught with turmoil almost from the beginning. White was abusive toward Aretha, although Franklin waited until the end of the decade before obtaining a divorce. She and White had their first and only child together, Ted White, Jr. ("Teddy"), in 1964. Her relationship with Teddy has proven better than with her ex-husband, as Teddy has provided musical accompaniment for his mother on a number of occasions. Aretha and Ted White stayed together through 1969, at which point a divorce was finalized. Franklin waited to remarry until 1978, when she married Glynn Turman (whom she divorced in 1984). Between 1968 and 1978, however, Aretha had romantic relationships and her third child, Kecalf Cunningham, was the result of her affair with Ken Cunningham (ironically enough, also a manager). Aretha and Ken arranged to get married, only for Aretha to cancel the wedding. Ultimately, the fact that Aretha has remained unmarried from 1984 through the present moment signals that she is perhaps happiest as a single woman.

If Columbia struggled to arrive at a successful niche for Aretha, this did not prevent them from releasing her music at a prolific rate. In 1962, the year after *Aretha*, two additional albums came out: *The Electrifying Aretha Franklin* and *The Tender, the Moving, the Swinging Aretha Franklin*. Between the two, the latter was the more successful, although it did not build on her first album. As the decade progressed, Franklin started to venture closer to the "pop" end of the spectrum, distancing herself from the gospel category. It must be noted that this was not Aretha's decision, but rather reflects the decision of John Hammond and Columbia. To an extent, their strategy paid off, as Aretha recorded "One Step Ahead" and "Cry Like a Baby" in 1965 and 1966 respectively, both of which garnered major commercial success. Her celebrity status was firmly intact, as she was earning six figures for her performances. However, in assessing Aretha Franklin's career with Columbia, one must recognize that while songs like "One Step Ahead" were successful in a vacuum, they fell well short of the kind of sales and acclaim that Aretha Franklin could achieve. It would not, in fact, be until 1967—after leaving Columbia—that Aretha would record her first chart-topping single.

Chapter 3: A Star In Her Own Right

"Music changes, and I'm gonna change right along with it." – Aretha Franklin

One of the great challenges that Aretha Franklin faced during the early stages of her career was the expectation that she would inherit the mantle from the successful African-American female performers who antedated her, including Billie Holiday and Dinah Washington. In the early-mid 1960s, Franklin began recording covers of songs devised by Washington; a development that Michael Awkward argues reflected an attempt to legitimize her music: "When Dinah Washington died in 1963, Franklin—a former child prodigy who, after her stirring debut in 1961, had produced a string of unremarkable albums—seemed unprepared to join the line of transcendent black female singers that includes Bessie Smith, Billie Holiday, and Ella Fitzgerald. Having been deemed 'the next one' by Washington herself, but having failed to that point to produce recordings that proved indisputably that she was worthy of such praise, Franklin's remakes of songs associated with the recently-deceased Queen of Blues can be seen as her attempt to demonstrate that she was indeed ready to wear her idol's crown."

Dinah Washington

Ultimately, covering Washington's music did nothing to advance her career, although this was largely due to the inability of Columbia to feature her properly. It would not be until closer to the end of the decade that she truly developed the kind of commercial viability that Washington predicted in anointing Aretha as "the next one."

The departure from Columbia had been a time coming, and while Ted White was a poor influence on Aretha outside of a personal context, he had been correct in reacting negatively to the way in which Aretha was used and marketed by Columbia. In January of 1967, Aretha signed with Atlantic Records and 1967 would prove to be the most successful year of her career to that point. Her first major event with Atlantic occurred that same month, when she went to Muscle Shoals, Alabama to record "I Never Loved a Man (The Way I Love You)," which was issued the following month. The song proved to be the one that launched Aretha's career to new levels, and Peter Winkler argues that the song succeeded through its open synthesis between gospel and pop: "'I Never Loved a Man' was the song that initiated Aretha Franklin's rise to stardom and hence represents a pivotal moment in the diffusion of Afro-American styles to a mass audience. Though she was not the first black artist to achieve success singing popular music in a Gospel-based style, Aretha Franklin was the first woman to do so, and her popularity with the mainstream pop audience eclipsed that of performers such as Clyde McPhatter, Sam Cooke, or even Ray Charles." (194)

McPhatter

The kind of marriage between gospel and rock that Winkler locates was precisely, of course, what Columbia had failed to achieve during the six years in which Franklin had been signed with them. From 1961-1967, Columbia had attempted to transform Aretha Franklin into a pop singer exclusively, and while she was certainly competent in this capacity, her gospel inclinations had lain dormant, thereby robbing her of a singular dimension of her vocal style.

Winkler also notes the manner in which Aretha Franklin broke away from the standards of her race (and more specifically, of her gender within her race). To be certain, there had been enormously successful female black vocalists, chief among them Billie Holiday. However, Holiday would never have been confused with a gospel singer, and she was far more invested in jazz than Franklin's more religiously-inflected (and less avant-garde) style. The great question that Franklin's career was tasked with resolving was whether gospel, a genre that was heavily religiously-charged and fundamental to black heritage, could succeed with a crossover audience. The answer, obviously, was yes, and 1967 proved to be the year that would begin demonstrating the crossover appeal of Aretha Franklin's gospel-pop music.

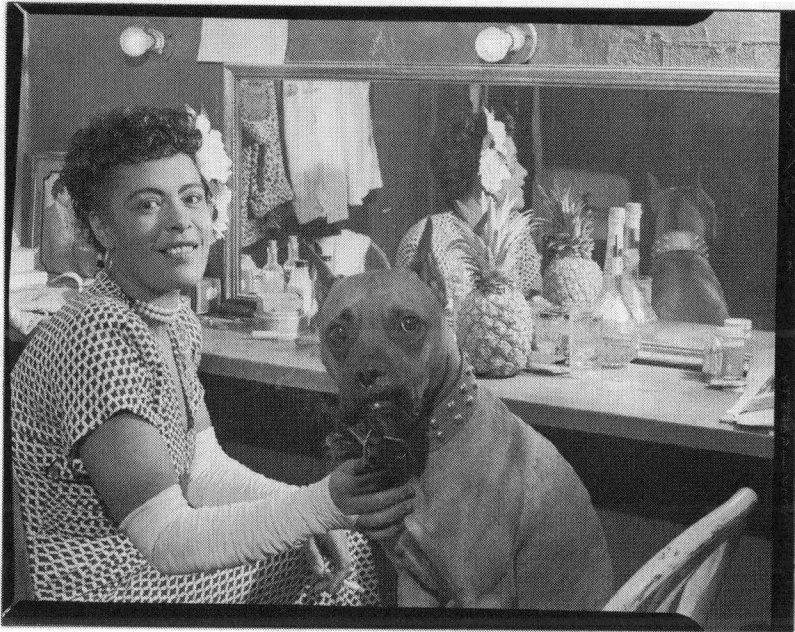

Billie Holiday

Listening to "I Never Loved a Man," it is not difficult to understand how the song has remained such an enduring classic. The song features deep chords that recall blues music, but slightly more over-the-top than the more modernist jazz style. The song is at once more formally experimental than most pop music, but with a punchy rhythm that satisfied the mainstream listener. Winkler contends that Franklin's music was in fact remarkably experimental on a formal level, stating, "Aretha Franklin's singing is another matter altogether. Her flexible molding of pitch, rhythm, and timbre bursts through the arbitrary confines of our notational system. It will be very difficult to represent what she is singing in terms of the tempered scale or unambiguous subdivisions of the beat." (186)

Franklin's music was formally experimental in a way that most pop music was not, but the gospel quality of the music was perhaps the riskiest quality of her style—this was, after all, the dimension that Columbia had been so reticent to foreground years while Franklin remained with them. This was a quality that distinguished Franklin from the emerging legion of African-American singers from Motown, with groups that included Martha and the Vandellas and The Supremes. These groups were enormously successful but without the kind of emotional gravitas that the gospel quality generated. In this respect, Franklin's music not only deviated from the kind of music that white audiences were accustomed to, but also from the kind of music that her African-American female contemporaries were performing.

Thus, "I Never Loved a Man" was the song that truly catapulted Aretha Franklin's career, and the b-side for the song, "Do Right Woman, Do Right Man," also performed quite well. Indeed, "I Never Loved a Man" reached the top position on the R&B charts, as well as number nine on the Billboard charts.

For all the success of these two songs, however, it was the song that she recorded later in 1967, "Respect" that remains her most enduring accomplishment. Even though Franklin's name is now virtually synonymous with "Respect," the song was actually a hit when Otis Redding (who also wrote the song) performed it in the 1950s. Franklin's version reached a level of popularity that Redding's version never achieved though, and it topped both the R&B and Billboard charts. The song is far more emotionally-charged than her two earlier hit songs with Atlantic, and Franklin sings with the kind of fervency that one imagines took place in the church services of Aretha's father. To be sure, the call-and-response rhythms of the song, in which Franklin sings in the foreground with a chorus echoing and responding to her, holds a filial relation to the dynamics of a singing performance within a church congregation. The song does not simply unfold, it pulsates, and with an energy that is easily the equal of the hits that were being released by her Motown brethren. In addition, one of the pleasures of listening to "Respect" is simply the sense of wonder generated by Franklin's remarkably fast vocal articulation. While Aretha Franklin would record more than 80 chart-placing singles, "Respect" remains the consensus pick for her most iconic song, and it is easy to understand why.

Otis Redding

Most discussions of "Respect" (and indeed, Aretha Franklin's music more generally) focus on the rhythms of her music, but one should not overlook the lyrics of "Respect," which were instrumental in the song achieving the cultural importance that it maintains. Contextualized within 1967 America, the title held profound implications on both race and gender levels. In this respect, it is worth noting that 1967 was the Summer of Love, the year before race riots reached unprecedented levels the following year. As such, in 1967 racial tensions were simmering and "Respect" participated in the activism that was being undertaken by Martin Luther King, Jr. and others. In performing "Respect," Franklin did not declare an expressly activist motivation for the song, but she was unafraid to express her support for the Civil Rights Movement.

As Buzzy Jackson noted, Aretha also emerged to prominence at a moment in United States cultural history in which the celebrity entertainer began enjoying greater cultural authority, to the point that they could effectively influence more people than ever before, not only through speaking engagements but—especially in the case of Franklin—their actual practice. Jackson explains, "For her part, Franklin was a lifelong supporter of King and his movement and considered herself a devoted partner in his fight. But something else had changed in American culture; the entertainer was becoming just as powerful as the politician." (174). Jackson's remark must be qualified with the fact that Franklin was not merely the beneficiary of a changing social landscape because she also participated in the change that took place through her music. Indeed, a song like "Respect" was effective in mobilizing the public toward racial equality, in the same manner as an explicit speaking demonstration.

In any event, Franklin's open support for the Civil Rights Movement distanced herself from many of the famous black musicians who had come before, including Louis Armstrong and Duke Ellington. Armstrong had been particularly susceptible to allegations that he was guilty of supporting the pejorative "Uncle Tom" stereotype of the domestic African-American, and the inadequacy of Armstrong and Ellington from a civil rights standpoint was only enhanced through the fact that much of their fame derived from the success they achieved while performing in all-white nightclubs. In contrast, with Aretha Franklin, one encountered a singer who was unafraid to lend support to the Civil Rights cause, doing so not only outside of her professional obligations but even through her artistic practice. Buzzy Jackson goes so far as to argue that in the wake of "Respect," "Aretha was suddenly the most compelling face of the Civil Rights Movement." (174). Whether or not one accepts this characterization (in 1967, Martin Luther King, Jr. was still alive, after all), it must be noted that Aretha was able to galvanize support for Civil Rights in a unique way through her art rather than through public speaking arrangements, and that this held a crossover appeal that extended well beyond the core demographic of her race.

One of the fascinating aspects of "Respect" is the way in which it supports both the racial change that Franklin wanted to see implemented, and also the emerging second-wave feminist movement. Following this interpretation, "Respect" refers to the need for women to become as respected as their male counterparts. Following this characterization, it is significant that the song itself was first written by a man (Otis Redding), with Franklin appropriating it. Contextualized within the historical moment of 1967 America, second-wave feminism was already well underway by the time Aretha recorded the song, and one can justifiably argue that the song participated in the movement in its own way (even though Franklin herself was reticent to expressly designate the song as a feminist text).

By 1967, Title VII of the Civil Rights Act had already been passed, which prohibited employment discrimination on the basis of one's gender (as well as race), and a year before "Respect," the National Organization for Women (NOW) was formed, with Betty Friedan leading the charge. Meanwhile, the same year that Aretha recorded the song, the birth control pill was featured on the cover of *TIME*. Andi Zeisler expounds upon the feminist subtext of "Respect": "By the 1970s, popular culture was quickly becoming both a locus for feminist organizing and a source of simmering empowerment…Aretha Franklin's 'Respect' took Otis Redding's 1950s hit and gave it a righteous gender flip. The so-called sexual revolution encouraged women to cast off their hang-ups, and a growing number of female writers, artists, musicians, and reporters instructed them how to do so." (55)

Friedan

Thus, just as race relations were making headlines and emerging to the fore of American culture, a parallel phenomenon was emerging in the domain of gender. One of the reasons that "Respect" remains such a significant cultural milestone is that it participated in both the gender and racial discourses of the moment, an example of the capacity for art to not only offer entertainment but also to participate in ideological debates and mobilize efforts for social change.

Chapter 4: The Queen

"Be your own artist, and always be confident in what you're doing. If you're not going to be confident, you might as well not be doing it." – Aretha Franklin

Although Aretha had been moderately successful during her time with Columbia, it was difficult to have foreseen the kind of success that she reached from the outset with Atlantic. If she went from underachieving pop singer to A-list celebrity more or less overnight, however, Aretha would prove quite adept in managing her celebrity, due to a plurality of factors. First of all, she benefitted from C.L.'s perspective, as her father had always been remarkably effective in building and maintaining his own celebrity. Second, Aretha had performed since her early teenage years and what she lacked in formal education, she compensated for through her show business experience. Finally, where many emerging celebrities are still in their teenage years and suffer from immaturity, Franklin was already 25 years of age by 1967 and a fully-grown woman. The impression one received when witnessing Aretha was of a mature woman who understood herself. It is true that Aretha has forever been reticent to discuss her early pregnancy, but Buzzy Jackson makes the astute observation that Aretha Franklin's music projects the identity of a mature and confident woman. Jackson notes that "Aretha Franklin may not have been a Bad Woman per se, but she was not innocent; she was a mature, experienced woman, and that came across in her music" (173). In other words, Franklin was not puritanical, and demonstrated that a woman could be experienced and still satisfy social standards for decency.

Thus, 1967 proved to be a landmark year for Aretha Franklin, and it likely stands as the most significant year of her career. Over that year alone, she switched from Columbia (with whom she had lasted for six, frustrating years) and recorded three of her most important songs, including "Respect," considered her crowning achievement. While 1967 is the most decorated year of her career, however, it was not an outlier, as Franklin maintained the commercial viability that she demonstrated in her first year with Atlantic. In 1968, she released two of her best-selling albums, *Lady Soul* and *Aretha Now*; as the title of the former makes evident, her singing persona had become inextricably tied to her roots in soul and gospel music. These two albums included some of Aretha's most decorated songs, including "Chain of Fools," "Ain't No Way," and "I Say a Little Prayer." During 1968, Franklin also began receiving more awards and designations for her achievements; in February, she earned her first Grammy Award (she would earn another one later in her career) for Best Female R&B Vocal Performance. Later in February, Aretha was honored by Martin Luther King, Jr. (just two months before his assassination), who presented her with the SCLC Drum Beat Award. Perhaps her greatest distinction yet occurred in June of 1968, when she donned the cover of *TIME*, a particularly rare feat for musicians. In short, Aretha Franklin had successfully transitioned from musical performer to cultural icon.

Aretha's output in 1969 was slightly less prolific than it had been during the previous two years. She would never again reach the feverish heights that she had achieved in 1967, a year in which she released three albums in total. Meanwhile, 1968 saw the release of two albums, while in 1969, Aretha released just one, *Soul '69*. The album was not quite as successful as her past few ones had been, although it still reached number 15 on the Billboard charts and was the top-selling R&B album of the year. At the time of its release, *Soul '69* was generally well-regarded, although it did contain a couple of songs that were not praised, including "Tracks of My Tears" and "Gentle on My Mind." Perhaps as a result of this, and because it is often overshadowed by the albums that immediately preceded it, the album is not often cited among Aretha Franklin's finest.

If 1969 represented something of a disappointment for Aretha, she rebounded the following year and the 1970s were generally a period of great flourishing for her. On a personal level, she finalized her divorce from Ted White in 1969 and the new decade corresponded with a fresh outlook on her life and career. In 1970, she released two enormously-successful albums, *This Girl's In Love with You* and *Spirit in the Dark*. The former performed slightly better with the public, but both were improvements over *Soul '69*. *This Girl's in Love with You* boasts "Share Your Love with Me," which reached the top position on the R&B charts and the number 13 position on the Billboard charts. The song is relatively versatile and has been successfully performed by singers as diverse as Bobby "Blue" Bland (who gave the original recording), Aretha, and Kenny Rogers. "Share Your Love with Me" contains a much slower tempo than "Respect," but, as with the earlier song, is guided by a call-and-response rhythm between Aretha and her chorus. The song was actually recorded by Aretha in 1969, but she would give high-profile performances of it through 1971.

While "Share Your Love with Me" was the most beloved song in its album, *This Girl's in Love with You* contains several famous songs. Around the turn of the decade, Aretha began incorporating a number of covers of pop songs; she had long been open to covering well-known songs, dating back to early in the previous decade, when she famously covered Dinah Washington songs. Her covers from 1970 were different in that she began covering well-known pop songs; if her earlier covers took jazz and gospel music and gentrified it, here she began taking pop music and infusing it with the rhythms of her youth. This approach is on full display in *This Girl's in Love with You*, in which Aretha included covers of the Beatles' "Eleanor Rigby" and "Let it Be," as well as "Son of a Preacher Man." One interesting note is that Franklin's rendition of "Let it Be" was actually released in advance of the Beatles' version, which was not released until March of 1970. In the end, "Let it Be" would not be among the more acclaimed songs in the album for Franklin, as her strongest songs are likely "Share Your Love with Me" (the key song in the album) followed by "Eleanor Rigby" and "Son of a Preacher Man." Released in January of 1970, *This Girl's in Love with You* would prove to be the highlight of the year, generating strong momentum for her career in the wake of the disappointment of 1969.

In addition to *This Girl's in Love with You*, Aretha released one additional well-received album in 1970, *Spirit in the Dark*. This album is most often remembered for including "Don't Play that Song (You Lied)" and the eponymous "Spirit in the Dark." Of the two, the former sold better, reaching the top spot on the R&B charts and the number 11 position on the Billboard charts. *Spirit in the Dark* ranks among Aretha Franklin's most acclaimed album, although one of the curiosities of Franklin's career is that the album actually did not perform particularly well at the time of its release. Unlike Aretha's earlier albums with Atlantic, the album itself failed to even place in the Billboard Top 20, even if it is now considered one of her very best albums.

Whatever disappointment may have resulted from *Spirit in the Dark* (commercially, that is), her next album was a tremendous success. After not releasing an album in 1971, her 1972 album *Young, Gifted and Black* garnered her a second Grammy Award. The title for the album stemmed from Nina Simone's song "To Be Young, Gifted and Black." The album is remembered for including the landmark songs "Border Song," A Brand New Me," and "Rock Steady," among others. *Young, Gifted and Black* reached the number 11 spot on the Billboard charts. As successful as her studio albums were, however, Aretha Franklin's greatest achievements from the early 1970s may well have been live performances that were subsequently released on record. The first of these was *Aretha Live at Fillmore West*, an album that included songs performed by Aretha during a three-day series at the Fillmore West concert hall, a legendary venue in San Francisco. The iconic performance included many of Aretha's most decorated songs to that point in her career, including a storied rendition of "Respect." Although the concert was predicated around honoring Aretha's greatest hits, Aretha also performed a series of her most beloved covers, including "Eleanor Rigby" and the Simon and Garfunkel hit "Bridge Over Troubled Water." This latter recording reached the top spot on the R&B charts, while the album as a whole made it to the number seven position. The album is a testament not only to Aretha's musical acumen, but to her ability to apply material that her colleagues in the music industry had already made famous and apply an original spin that was definitively "Aretha's."

Nina Simone

Releasing the album of Aretha's concert series at the Fillmore West proved to be one of the best decisions that Atlantic ever made, and the company released another live performance of Aretha's the following year, titled *Amazing Grace* (1972). While *Aretha Live at Fillmore West* leaned slightly more heavily in the direction of pop, this latter album perched more squarely in the domain of gospel (as suggested by the title). *Amazing Grace* remains the best-selling album that Aretha has released over her entire career and the album earned Double Platinum status. The album is headlined by Aretha's rendition of the title song, but also includes classic songs that include "Mary Don't You Weep," "God Will Take Care of You," and "Take My Hand, Precious Lord." With *Amazing Grace*, Aretha returned to her roots, and the album both demonstrates her facility with gospel music and hints at the kind of material that she might have released had she devoted herself more exclusively to gospel music across her entire career. At the same time, one also wonders whether the album would have performed so well had Aretha not established herself as a crossover talent. In other words, much of the novelty of *Amazing Grace* derived from watching a pop-gospel singer return to her native genre, and the album performed particularly well because she was able to draw on a demographic that she had already won over through her work outside of gospel. In any event, the album was recorded from her performance at New Temple Missionary Baptist Church in Los Angeles, with the performance and recording taking place in January of 1972. With a running time of nearly one-and-a-half hours, *Amazing Grace* comprises one of the lengthiest of Franklin's albums and has sold more than two million copies in the United States. Curiously, it would be the last of Aretha's live albums until 1987.

Following the success of *Amazing Grace*, Aretha released just one album in 1973, *Hey Now Hey (The Other Side of the Sky)*. The album fared the poorest of Aretha's albums with Atlantic up to this point, barely missing the top 25 (finishing at number 30). *Hey Now Hey* remains one of the most polarizing of all of Aretha's albums, with a core of fans who embrace it. Yet, the album was regarded more ambivalently by the critical establishment. Even among those who felt that *Hey Now Hey* was one of the weakest of Aretha's albums, however, one of the songs, "Angel," stands as one of the very strongest of her career.

The highlight of 1973 for Aretha Franklin was the release of "Until You Come to Me (That's What I'm Gonna Do), a song that reached the number one spot on the R&B charts and the third position on the Billboard charts. As with so many of Aretha Franklin's songs, she was not the first to record the tune, as Stevie Wonder had recorded his iteration of it six years earlier. However, Wonder had not released it and would not do so until 1977, well after Aretha's version hit the public. Franklin's version now stands as the most famous recorded by any artist. The lyrics, which chronicle a spurned lover's attempt to win back their spouse, are a perfect site through which Aretha could project her somewhat over-the-top performing style. In this vein, Robert Christgau has noted that Aretha's rather bombastic performing style challenged distinctions between proper and improper taste, and that "Aretha Franklin's great gift is her voice, but her genius is her bad taste. Admirers who try to ignore who affronts ordinary notions of vocal decorum only prove that love is deaf" (100). If Franklin's style did not comport with traditional notions of taste politics, however, this only strengthened her appeal and songs like "Until You Come to Me" are among the most beloved of her career. In outdoing Stevie Wonder in his version of the same material, Franklin also not only demonstrated her ability to outperform a major singer of the hegemonic gender, but it also demonstrated her talent for covering a song and making the material entirely her own.

By the early-mid 1970s, Aretha Franklin was firmly entrenched as one of the most decorated singers in America, regardless of genre. With this visibility, of course, came pressure to conform to the prevailing body image standards of American culture, and this was particularly challenging for Aretha. Specifically, Franklin had always been a large woman, which stood in marked contrast with the uber-thin profile that grew to prominence in the 1960s. As noted earlier, Aretha had always managed her celebrity quite effectively, due to her strong will and a support system anchored by her father, but she felt pressure to lose weight and for the rest of her career, Aretha's weight has remained an aspect of her celebrity that surfaces quite often in media coverage of her. During the early 1970s, Aretha went on an extreme crash diet that saw her lose a few dozen pounds. As with many crash diets, however, she quickly regained the weight. According to David Ritz, Aretha's weight fluctuates with the vicissitudes of her disposition; when in times of great stress, she has a tendency to overeat. In any event, from the early 1979s-onward, Franklin's weight has undergone rather dramatic shifts and she has been open in discussing her dieting and the challenges of maintaining a healthy weight.

Chapter 5: Career Challenges and Diva Status

"I've been around long enough for people to know who I am and what my contributions are. They know me as more than just an artist. I think they know me as a woman as well." – Aretha Franklin

By the middle of the decade, Aretha Franklin had been a major star in the record industry for the better part of a decade and successfully synthesized the gospel music of her youth with the broader category of pop music. Her talent was recognized not only through her chart-topping sales but also through the multiple Grammy Awards with which she had been honored. If the first half of the decade saw her more or less continue the success that she established beginning in 1967, the latter half of the decade was not as kind to Aretha and she has never quite regained the commercial and critical success enjoyed during her golden years. A challenging development was the departure from Atlantic of music producer Jerry Wexler. Despite his absence, Aretha continued to release albums at a prolific rate, but the critical and commercial success of them became increasingly sporadic.

The most significant venture for Aretha in 1976 actually concerned her involvement in a motion picture—a medium in which she had hesitated to become involved with to that point in her career. Rather than acting in the picture, however, she assisted with the soundtrack. This fact is rather ironic considering that the narrative of the film is inspired by the Supremes, a rival Motown group to Aretha Franklin. In any event, while Aretha did not actually star in the movie, she was responsible for the film's highlight, the song "Something He Can Feel," which she performed for the soundtrack. The lengthy song (spanning more than six minutes) was a terrific hit, reaching the top spot on the R&B charts. Surprisingly enough, this would prove to be the final top-40 hit of the decade for Franklin.

The last few years of the decade were unkind to Aretha. In 1977, she recorded *Sweet Passion*, an album that might be said to have directed her career in an unfortunate direction (it was her worst-performing record with Atlantic). Aretha had reason to expect the album to be successful, as she paired with notable Motown producer Lamont Dozier, but the fruits of their collaboration were mediocre. One of the songs, "Break It To Me Gently," peaked at number 85 on the Billboard charts and reached number one on the R&B charts, but the album as a whole performed miserably. Unlike other albums of Aretha's that did not perform particularly well at the time of their release, the critical reception of *Sweet Passion* has not improved with age.

One year after *Sweet Passion*, Aretha released *Almighty Fire*, still with Atlantic, but it fared even worse. Released in May of 1978, Aretha worked with producer Curtis Mayfield on the album; she had worked with Mayfield in recording the soundtrack for *Sparkle*, but this effort was a great disappointment. Finally, in 1979 Aretha made one final effort for Atlantic, recording *La Diva*. The album, Aretha's 27th in total, would comprise the last that she would record for Atlantic and was a massive disappointment. Although its lack of success continued a trend that had been established during the last couple of years, *La Diva* had actually signaled an attempt on Franklin's part to diversify into a new category. Specifically, by the mid-late 1970s it was clear that the hybrid of pop and gospel that Aretha had perfected (and which hit the cultural sweet spot during the late 1960s and early 1970s) had been superseded by disco. *La Diva* was Aretha's attempt at a disco album, but the results were unconvincing and she would not return to this terrain. In fact, it would be several years before Aretha was able to mount a successful professional comeback.

Before the end of the decade, Aretha married her second husband, the actor Glynn Turman. They were married on April 11, 1978, at C.L.'s church. The marriage also meant that Aretha was to become stepmother to Turman's three children from a previous marriage. However, the marriage was no more successful than her first one and she and Turman separated in 1982, although it would not be until 1984 that they actually concretized a divorce. Aretha has not been married since, although she has been involved in high-profile relationships over the past 30 years.

Turman

With the disappointment of *La Diva*, it was clear that Aretha Franklin needed to move in a new direction (one that did not involve disco, either) and she signed with Arista Records. The most important event of the year was not a record release but rather Aretha's performance at the Royal Albert Hall, with Queen Elizabeth in attendance. That same year, she also made the sharp decision to appear in *The Blues Brothers* (1980), a film that was simultaneously a parody and celebration of gospel and blues music. The film boasted not only Aretha (in the role of a waitress) but also Ray Charles, in addition to John Belushi and Dan Aykroyd having the starring roles. Acting in *The Blues Brothers* not only reflected Aretha's status as royalty within her musical genre but also displayed her ability to poke fun at herself and her musical category. That the film was a box office hit also redirected her career, generating positive momentum that had been sorely lacking during the few years prior.

The first album that Aretha Franklin released for Arista was *Aretha*, which came out in 1980. That the album was titled *Aretha* reflected the effort on the part of Arista to construct a new beginning for her career, as "Aretha" had also been the title of her first album with Columbia, which had itself marked a new beginning away from the exclusively-gospel music she had performed during the first several years of her career. The album was highlighted by the inclusion of "United Together," a song that reached number three on the R&B charts. The album as a whole returned to the gospel-inflected rhythms of Franklin's most acclaimed work, successfully re-igniting her career. In addition to "United Together," *Aretha* contained another cover of an Otis Redding classic, "I Can't Turn You Loose." Even if it did not reach the heights of "Respect" (her more well-known cover of Redding), Aretha's rendition of "I Can't Turn You Loose" was nominated for a Grammy and satisfied both Aretha's fan base and the general public as well.

The early 1980s proved to be successful, sustaining and even building on the triumph that had been *Aretha*. Her next album, *Love All the Hurt Way*, was released in 1981 and featured a memorable duet with George Benson. An even greater success was *Jump to It*, from 1982. The album topped the R&B charts and made it to number 23 on the Billboard charts. The title song remains one of Aretha's late-career highlights, a veritable tour de force that was nominated for a Grammy Award. The song wastes no time in establishing a fast beat, recalling the dynamic rhythms of "Respect" in certain respects. Where "Respect" was more defined by its famous lyrics, however, one senses that "Jump to It" is driven more by its rhythm than its lyrics. The song feels very much a product of the 1980s, producing an almost kinesthetic response in the listener that made it perfect for aerobics classes (almost in the vein of Michael Jackson's famous hits from the same decade).

The year after *Jump to It*, Franklin recorded *Get It Right*, which received a mixed reception. One the one hand, the album was highlighted by the title song, which rose to the number one slot on the R&B charts. At the same time, though, the album as a whole fared not nearly as well, selling only around 200,000 copies. That the album performed so far below its expectations was particularly surprising in light of the fact that Aretha collaborated with producer Luther Vandross in making it, the same producer with whom she had worked on the highly-acclaimed *Jump to It* just one year earlier. The wide gulf in critical reception between the two albums only reinforces the unpredictable vicissitudes of Franklin's career.

Luther Vandross and Diana Ross

In the wake of *Jump to It*, Aretha regained momentum quickly, performing quite well at mid-decade. Her next album following *Get It Right* was *Who's Zoomin' Who?*, one of the finest albums Aretha Franklin ever released. Franklin would be quick to distance herself from sentiments that the album represented a comeback, and she was only "coming back" from one poor album from two years earlier. Still, in the popular narrative of her career, the album is considered to have resurrected her career; in his assessment of the album, Mark Bego claimed, "Not only did the disc serve as a treat for the legion of her fans from the 1960s, but its hot, fresh, sassy sound also captured a new audience of young record buyers who had previously considered her a nostalgic legend of days gone by" (236). Despite Bego's claims, to anyone who has listened to Aretha Franklin's music from each chapter of her career, there is no doubt that *Who's Zoomin' Who?* stands in marked contrast with the music that Aretha performed early in her career. Her voice is still powerful, but by the mid-1980s, she began relying more heavily on the intervention of studio-produced effects to enhance her vocals (Ritz). Aretha, for her part, was quick to celebrate the album, considering it among her very best.

One year after *Who's Zoomin' Who?*, Franklin recorded *Aretha*, her third album bearing her name as its title. The album is most remembered for featuring a remarkable duet with Franklin and George Michael, with the song reaching the number position not only on the R&B charts but also the Billboard charts as well. Aretha also continued to display her facility with covering famous songs, performing a memorable rendition of the famous Rolling Stones song "Jumpin' Jack Flash." The album cover is also quite striking, featuring Aretha in the Pop aesthetic of Andy Warhol—this was the final work that he produced before his untimely death the following year. In any event, *Aretha* is perhaps the crowning achievement of late-career Aretha Franklin and ranks alongside the finest work of her career.

An issue with designating *Who's Zoomin' Who?* as Aretha's "comeback" album is that it suggests that a period of sustained success occurred in its wake, and this was not the case. Indeed, *Who's Zoomin' Who?* represents the final hit album for Aretha Franklin until *A Rose is Still a Rose* more than one decade later. In 1989, *Through the Storm* performed quite poorly, despite the fact that the title song involved a duet between Aretha and Elton John. As disappointing as *Through the Storm* was, it actually generated more sales than her next album, *What You See is What You Sweat*, the last album she would record until *A Rose is Still a Rose*. In his assessment of the album, Bego contends that it offers more than it has been given credit for, and that "If the songs are uneven, they don't prevent the Queen of Soul [Franklin] from exuberantly expressing the breadth of her musical personality, from regal pop-gospel diva to funky everyday person" (302). There may be merit to this appreciative critique, but the low sales led to an extended hiatus.

Chapter 6: Staying Power

Aretha receiving the Presidential Medal of Freedom in 2005

"Don't say Aretha is making a comeback, because I've never been away!" – Aretha Franklin

By the late-1990s, not only was Aretha Franklin well into her middle-age years, but she had gone more than a decade since recording a hit album. She had remained active, largely through her involvement in movie soundtracks, including the score for the hit (and important film from a racial standpoint) Spike Lee film *Malcolm X* (1993). That she and Arista opted to produce a greatest hits album in 1994 speaks to the fact that there was a prominent sentiment that Aretha's best years were already in the past. Still, the long hiatus since her last major original album would change in 1998, with the release of *A Rose is Still a Rose*. The album was headlined by the song of the same name, and the album is easily the great achievement of the 1990s for Aretha. Not only was she nominated for a Grammy award for Best R&B Album, but for Best R&B Song (the title song) as well. As with Franklin's best music, the album managed to not only satisfy fans of Aretha's soul music, but also the younger generation more invested in pop music.

While *A Rose is Still a Rose* emphatically demonstrated the enduring commercial and critical viability of Aretha Franklin, the album did not lead to her renewing the kind of workload that she had maintained across most of her career. In fact, it would be a full five years before her next album, *So Damn Happy*, which she completed at the age of 61 (in 2003.) By this time, Franklin had quit smoking, a decision necessary in order to save her voice, although quitting cigarettes did lead to extreme weight gain. In any event, listening to *So Damn Happy*, one gets no sense of a voice that has become tired and the album was well-received. In the narrative of her career, there is a way in which it stands as a bittersweet event, as it with this album that Aretha announced her departure from Arista (she would record one additional album in 2007, *Jewels in the Crown: All-Star Duets with the Queen*, but her relationship with the company was effectively over by that point. The company saw Aretha produce some of her best work, and while her output and the reception of her works during her time with Arista was somewhat erratic, the partnership with Arista was certainly preferable to her time with Columbia during the formative years of her career.

Even after clearing the 60 years of age hurdle, Aretha remained active professionally, both performing live and recording. In 2008, her first album after separating from Arista was produced, *This Christmas, Aretha*. As the name would suggest, the album included an array of Christmas favorites, chief among them "'Twas the Night Before Christmas," "Silent Night," and "Angels We Have Heard on High." This album offers compelling renditions of famous Christmas songs, although it is valuable more in the nostalgic vein than in marking any new direction for her career. The more notable event of the past several years involved Aretha's performance in 2009 at President Barack Obama's inaugural ceremony, as she sang a spirited rendition of "My Country 'Tis of Thee." For the occasion, Aretha donned a church hat, and the performance marked a return to Aretha aligning herself with the kind of politically-motivated activity that characterized much of her activity in the 1960s (during the concurrent Second-Wave Feminism and the Civil Rights Movements). It made perfect sense that Aretha would be selected to perform for Obama, as Franklin's presence brought Obama's inauguration in conversation with the cultural milieu of the Civil Rights Movement. In addition, Aretha had never shied away from professing her commitment to the Democratic Party, so the performance saw Aretha not only perform as Franklin the famous singer, but Franklin the committed Democrat as well.

(Aretha Singing at Obama's 2009 Inauguration)

The past several years have seen Aretha bestowed with honors and distinction, including honorary degrees from both Yale University and Harvard University. Her health has suffered, however. As noted earlier, Aretha managed to successfully quit smoking, but in 2010 she suffered from a tumor that caused her to cancel a slew of concerts. Her health treatments led to a hiatus, but Franklin returned to performing in 2011. However, two years later, in 2013, she was forced to cancel performing engagements in order to undergo another medical procedure. It would not be until December of 2013 that she would return to performing. The following year fared better, as she gave a series of performances. It is also worth noting that Aretha has not retired from recording albums, and another one is in the production process. Despite approaching 75 years of age, Franklin has demonstrated little intention of retiring and one senses that she will stay active for the rest of her life. At this point, Aretha has outlived her older sister Erma (who passed away in 2002) and younger sister Carolyn (who died quite young, in 1988). Her health has been a cause for concern in recent years, although access to strong medical care has facilitated successful recoveries. Despite the fact that Aretha continues to record new material, it is difficult to believe that her career will chart any new directions over the coming years. The fact that Aretha Franklin continues to actively perform is likely cause enough for her fans to be content, and Franklin's significance as an American culture figure is well-established.

Aretha at a memorial for Martin Luther King, Jr. in 2011

When Aretha Franklin burst onto the music scene, Motown had yet to establish itself as a music mecca. Indeed, it would be a number of years before African-American music was able to diversify, expanding (but not breaking away from entirely) the religiously-inflected category of gospel music. Franklin would herself play a fundamental role in effecting the transformation that brought gospel music into the mainstream, with a synthesis between the traditional gospel music and the more secular rhythms of pop music. This biography has also explicated the way in which this shift involved a dramatic turn away from the music of her youth, although she benefitted from the savvy business acumen of her father as well. Moreover, Aretha's accomplishments are not limited to aesthetic or formal developments within and across musical genres. Following the lead of her father, from the start of her career she has embraced the opportunity to become a leader in the African-American community (and Democratic Party, more recently), making her an icon of the Civil Rights Movement and an enduring presence during the political campaigns of President Obama. To this end, Aretha's career evidences an inseparability between music and politics that ensures her standing as not only an important musician but also a cultural icon as well.

As she advances through her seventies, Aretha Franklin's career remains active but it is unlikely that great innovations will follow; to watch Aretha perform in person is to honor the career that she has achieved, not to expect new directions. With an array of health problems in recent years, Franklin's performing schedule has grown rather unpredictable, but she still remains more prolific than the majority of singers her age, many of whom are retired. As she progresses through her advanced years, Aretha Franklin remains a valuable presence not only for what she represented during the prime of her career but for the connection she has established with younger generations of fans as well.

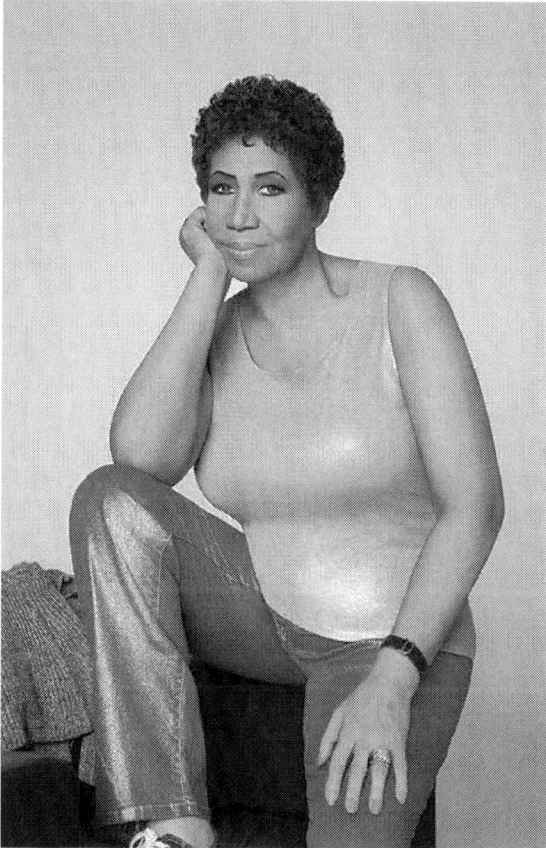

Sony Music portrait of Aretha in 2014

Stevie Wonder

Chapter 1: Childhood

"Mama was my greatest teacher, a teacher of compassion, love and fearlessness. If love is sweet as a flower, then my mother is that sweet flower of love." – Stevie Wonder

Born Stevland Hardaway Judkins, May 13, 1950 in Saginaw, Michigan, not far from the city of Detroit, the man who would begin his career as "Little Stevie Wonder" was born to Calvin Judkins and Lulu Mae Hardaway. He was born six weeks premature, and for various medical and procedural reasons, entirely blind. The most prevailing claim is that he "received too much oxygen in the incubator as a premature baby,"[278] resulting in a condition known as *retinopathy of prematurity* "because the blood vessels at the back of his eyes had not yet reached the front…an aborted growth spurt [that] caused his retinas to detach."[279]

Wonder's father is said to have been an abusive sort, and was not, in the long run, to figure into his son's life with any lasting significance. His mother, Lulu Mae Hardaway, a songwriter from Alabama who had been forced into the marriage, and into a life of prostitution by a significantly older husband, left Judkins and moved with her three sons to Detroit while Stevland was still in early childhood. There, she changed her son's name to Stevland Morris, and took every step imaginable to prevent continued contact with her former husband and the boy's father.

As is the case with many artists' mothers, Lula Mae Hardaway sensed, even during her son's early childhood, that a glimmer of talent was making itself known, before others were aware of it. A similar thing would occur in Marvin Gaye's and Michael Jackson's families as well, and Lulu Hardaway's family was to be no exception. Her first impulse was to find a cure for her son's blindness, and she left no avenue uninvestigated, even taking him to see the famous evangelist, Oral Roberts, in hopes that a sight-saving miracle might take place. Despite the failure of that meeting, the miracle occurred soon after, when Stevie developed an uncanny and immediate affinity for every new musical instrument he touched over the next few years, "all of which he taught himself before age 10,"[280] including harmonica, piano, and drums, among other instruments, all at a high performance level. His fearlessness at conquering new challenges would, in time, lead him to experiment with the new era's most cutting-edge electronic instruments, some of them still off-putting to many of his colleagues, and in large part due to such curiosity, he would lead the overall music industry into the synthesizer age, a multi-capacity instrument that has led to a new world of sampled and merged sounds in today's studios, for recording, live performance, and film.

A powerful force in vast international humanitarian projects, Stevie Wonder is and always has been politically liberal by nature, and is generally prone to the position of a pacifist, "a lifelong advocate of nonviolent political change," after the manner of Gandhi and King. His entire

---

[278] Bio.Com, Stevie Wonder Biography

[279] Encyclopaedia Brittanica, Stevie Wonder – www.britannica.com/EBchecked/topics/647209/Stevie-Wonder

[280] Bio.Com, Stevie Wonder Biography

musical output easily crosses racial lines, as he seems to take little apparent interest in disunity, and his broad outreach has, from the beginning, "epitomized sixties utopianism."[281] Such an expansive point of view has resulted in countless outreach collaborations with the world's greatest fellow musicians. In terms of central career goals, however, Wonder was not inattentive, and won fifteen Grammy awards in the decade of the 70s alone, with a regimen of innovative and well-produced works through personal perfectionism. Well into the twenty-first century, his music is still a moving force within the industry, even though he records and performs at a somewhat less frantic pace than in the past.

With the challenge of blindness, Wonder was less active in outdoor activities common to childhood, and he once noted, "When I was a child, kids used to make fun of me because I was blind. But I just became more curious, 'How can I climb this tree and get an apple for this girl?' That's what mattered to me." At the same time, however, being forced indoors likely hastened the remarkable progress made in his early music education. His understandably protective mother was careful to nourish his passion for music, and as so many artists did, Wonder spent the formative years of childhood singing in the church choir. Eventually, however, school years bring a parallel experience in secular music in most cases, and Wonder soaked this in the introduction to unknown secular forms as avidly as he had the weekly dose of gospel music, expressed in a style that would mark his later performing days as highly distinctive.

Wonder was discovered in this protected environment by Gerald White, brother of soul singer Ron White, who was eventually convinced to come and meet the boy and his mother. Apparently impressed with what he saw and heard, a meeting was arranged with Motown's executive and founder, Berry Gordy, when Wonder was around the age of 10, not an easy meeting to arrange or an easy audition to take on for an inexperienced youth.

[281] Stevie Wonder, Stevie Wonder Biography

Angela George's picture of Berry Gordy

Despite the extraordinary relationship the two would enjoy in later years, Wonder's audition did not, at first, unfold as the fairy tale that White, Wonder and his mother might have preferred. The CEO of Motown, who specialized in discovering and promotion talented children, was entirely unimpressed with the boy's singing, and equally unenthused about his skill on either the drums or the bongos. However, Wonder had developed an unorthodox and exciting style at the harmonica, often considered as merely a peripheral instrument, and the audition succeeded based on the fact that Gordy seemed fascinated with this new sort of "frantic harmonica playing,"[282] so he signed the child at once to a Motown contract in 1961 for his ability to play and sing at the same time. For promotional purposes, Stevie Hardaway Morris became Little Stevie Wonder, a name and public image intended to represent a perfect childhood bookend to the legendary blind artist Ray Charles. The name came about from a revelatory moment in which Gordy characterized Wonder's musical persona as "a little wonder."

---

[282] Encyclopaedia Britannica, Stevie Wonder

Eric Koch's picture of Ray Charles

Chapter 2: Early Years at Motown

"You know, I always when people ask me, like, what is my most favorite song, I quote Duke Ellington, when they would ask him, what's his favorite composition? And I say, I haven't written it yet. Because, you know, there are different songs for different occasions." – Stevie Wonder

 The preparation for the newest member of Motown began immediately, and within a short time, Wonder was "groomed…for Motown stardom."[283] However, even for the expert Gordy, finding a niche for the boy artist proved to be difficult at first, and the studio struggled to find the perfect fit. Wonder's first three years in the music industry were spent as "an R&B screamer in the Ray Charles mode."[284] The 'young screamer' model resulted in the release of two albums, beginning with "The Jazz Soul of Little Stevie" in 1961, released in 1962 on the Tamla label, and was immediately followed by the "Tribute to Uncle Ray," recorded at the age of 11 and released at 12. "Jazz" is the only one of Wonder's albums on which he does not sing. Based on his initial impressions of the boy, Gordy figured that Wonder would probably not become a viable singing artist in the style of a balladeer or as a soothing soul sound, so the "semi-sprechstimme" (as much spoken as sung) style of Ray Charles seemed the clear path at the time. "A tribute to Uncle Ray" was the second album released.

---

[283] Rolling Stone, Stevie Wonder Biography
[284] Rolling Stone, Stevie Wonder Biography

As Wonder grew, however, and his voice began to change, so did the minds of the Motown management. Within the third year, Gordy began to realize that his childhood creation, Little Stevie Wonder (who was becoming decreasingly little by the day), would become "much more than a freakish prepubescent imitation of Ray Charles."[285] Early mentors at the studio included bassist James Jamerson and drummer Benny Benjamin, musicians who would assist Wonder, to guide his natural instincts into the styles of his chosen genre, and to teach him the ways of the studio, which were to become an essential part of his world for the next half-century.

Jamerson

In 1963, Wonder released his first hit song, "Fingertips - Parts 1 and 2," reaching the top of the

---

[285] Rolling stone, Stevie Wonder Biography

Billboard charts, and providing the young artist with the first simultaneous hit single and album, "Recorded Live: The Twelve Year Old Genius," released in 1963, the first non-studio example to reach #1 on the charts. The spot where "Fingertips, part 2" begins is anecdotally designated as that spot in the music where Wonder is heard to shout, "Everybody say yeah!" Wonder played several of the percussion instruments, although a young Marvin Gaye can be heard on drums. Wonder was not quite 13 years of age when the album was recorded live at Chicago's Regal Theater, and an interesting account of the session reveals a state of pandemonium that took hold of the supporting musicians when Wonder took up the harmonica. The veterans are said to have had great difficulty in keeping up with the young virtuoso, and on the recording, one musician can be heard to shout repeatedly, "What key, what key?"

Marvin Gaye

As Wonder's image changed, as guided by Motown, his career began to take a clearer shape. It was noted by higher-ups at the studio that although the early singles had not produced the level of sales to the degree that everyone had hoped, Wonder was nothing short of sensational in live performances. In 1964, he fared equally well on the big screen, appearing in the debut movie, *Muscle Beach Party* and its sequel, *Bikini Beach*. In the latter classic, filmed during the Frankie Avalon and Annette Funicello craze, he sang "Happy Street" and "Happy Feeling (Dance and Shout)."

By the age of 14, nature began to take its course at a more rapid rate, and Wonder's voice began to change significantly. This was a critical moment in the transition from a child star to adult singer, a time at which not even the most astute vocal pedagogue can tell precisely what the new voice will sound like after adolescence. The larger question, in the minds of the studio staff - whether this new sound would attract a wide audience - had to be asked all over again, as if Wonder was a newly created artist. A second and equally immediate problem was apparent in the fact that the songs being written for Wonder by Clarence Paul were now set too high, and sat outside of Wonder's functional vocal range. Further, the young man had become increasingly interested in songwriting, and he began to compose a series of hits for himself and others within the studio. "Uptight (It's Alright)" and "With a Child's Heart" were particularly successful, as was "Tears of a Clown," written for Smokey Robinson & the Miracles. The singing regimen continued unabated as well, and Wonder's cover of Bob Dylan's "Blowin' in the Wind" would, in time, come to be considered one of the epic hit's best versions.

A sizeable segment of 1964 was spent in touring with The Rolling Stones, and in retrospect, Wonder would consider this time as an essentially valuable education, not only for purposes of learning the ins and outs of touring, but in sensing the structure and performance style of the music itself. More narrowly pigeonholed by Motown, his time with the Rolling Stones greatly widened his analytical understanding and appreciation for the closely-related genre for which the band was iconic, and greatly "broadened his awareness of rock and roll."[286] In the same year, Wonder covered "Heaven Help Us," and wrote the successful "It's a Shame" for the Motown Spinners.

As a play-off on the beach theme from the two movies, Motown released "Stevie at the Beach," the fourth album for Wonder on the Tamla label, issued in June, and featuring a minor hit, "Hey, Harmonica Man." The word "little" was to soon become conspicuously absent from Wonder's promotion. His voice was deepening further, and with his physique well on its way to a height of over six feet, the term made less sense with each concert and release. By the beginning of 1965, any thoughts of Wonder as a half-narrating and bellowing vocal artist had disappeared as well, and he would go on to release songs such as the smooth "My Cherie Amour" in the late '60s, to go along with songs recorded earlier but only now being released, including "Nothing's Too Good for My Baby" and the 1966 issue of hit single "Uptight Everything's Alright," written for Wonder's lower tenor voice.

By 1967, Wonder had not only become a seasoned adult performer but had also expanded his collaborations among colleagues in closely related genres based on his experiences with The Rolling Stones. In that same year, Wonder worked in London with The Jimi Hendrix Experience, playing drums, writing and covering for the London Sessions recorded by the BBC. Wonder had actually jammed with Hendrix previously, around the age of 17. While sitting at the drums, waiting for a BBC interview, Hendrix came in and a spontaneous session ensued on the song "Jammin'" and an instrumental version of Wonder's "I Was Made to Love Her." Video footage exists of the meeting, which was to come out later on the BBC sessions in 1998. Important

---

[286] Rock and Roll Hall of Fame, Stevie Wonder Biography – www.rockhall.com/inductees/stevie-wonder/bio

covers during the time with The Jimi Hendrix Experience included "I Was Made to Love Her" and "Someday at Christmas."

A picture from the Dutch National Archives of Wonder performing in the Netherlands in 1967

Wonder's regimen was similarly prolific in 1968, a year in which he co-wrote half of the music, and co-produced several of the tracks for the album, "For Once in My Life," which included a number of singles that went on to a top ten rating, such as "Shoo-Be-Doo-Be-Doo-Da-Day," "You Met Your Match," "I Don't Know Why," and "Yesterday Me, Yester-you, Yesterday." The album, along with the landmark "Cherie Amour," was released within the following year.

What took place in 1970 seemed typical of Motown artists who reached a high degree of artistic maturity and popularity. Wonder, like Jackson and Gaye, developed a fierce urge to innovate, experiment, and expand, only to come up against the Motown formula, which was understandably designed to produce maximum profit through prolific record sales and stellar chart ratings, not to grow artistically-realized and personally-fulfilled artists eager to develop the limits of their talents. In Wonder's case, he was "virtually self-sufficient in the studio,"[287] whether as a singer, producer, arranger, or instrumentalist and was already writing at a steady rate with his new wife, Syreeta Wright. With her support, he went off the Motown grid and model, recording two independent albums almost entirely without external assistance and without Berry Gordy's knowledge. One of the major hits of 1970 included "Signed, Sealed, Delivered", on which Wonder and his mother collaborated on the text. It was to be his first project with backup females, including his wife Syreeta, Venetta Fields, and Lynda Tucker Lawrence. The soul single spent six weeks in the #1 spot on the charts and earned Wonder his first Grammy nomination. 1970 also saw the release of "Heaven Help Us", composed by Ron Miller but first performed by Wonder with a touch of gospel directly taken from the experience of his upbringing and covered by artists such as Joan Baez and Ike and Tina Turner.

Syreeta continued to be a source of impetus for Wonder's ongoing innovations. Originally an aspiring ballet dancer who found that she couldn't afford the training, she worked as a secretary for Motown, and eventually as a songwriter at the suggestion of Wonder himself. In time, Wright was to become a Grammy-nominated singer who had caught Gordy's attention some time before. As with other Motown artists, the studio head was searching for the right spot in which he could most successfully promote her. Changing her name to Rita, he almost used her to replace Diana Ross of the Supremes, but eventually chose Jean Terrell instead. When he changed his mind and sought to place Wright with the Supremes again, the group rejected the notion, and by a vote, chose Terrell as the permanent member. Wonder's marriage to Syreeta would last only 18 months, but collaborations and conversations would continue through the years. One of the early successes in the collaboration included the song "It's a Shame," specifically for The Spinners. She co-wrote "Signed, Sealed and Delivered" with Wonder, Lee Garrett, and Wonder's mother, Lulu Mae Hardaway. Following the divorce less than two years later, she moved on to live in Ethiopia for a time as a meditation teacher, and she also converted to Islam. The two continued to exchange ideas, however, and she would appear on his album "Hotter Than July," released some years later, in the song "As If You Read My Mind."

Gordy was shocked by such an independent move by Wonder and the long-loyal Syreeta. Artists who brought lesser contributions to the studio would likely have been shown the door by the demanding and testy Motown CEO, and Wonder's struggle with the studio was not to be the only case by any stretch. Fellow artist Marvin Gaye would fight a stalemate of several months before returning to Motown with new guidelines, and Michael Jackson, with most of the Jackson

[287] Rolling Stone, Stevie Wonder Biography

family, simply severed relations and moved on in a tremendous leap of faith.

In Wonder's case, the overall atmosphere was, perhaps, less bitter over the long run than in the other two examples, and had not yet reached such an extreme negativity that would make the relationship irreparable. Still, the collision between a time-tested company formula, its founder, and a need to develop further artistically was significant, and lasted for some time, creating "a period of estrangement in the 70s."[288] Wonder and Gordy argued incessantly over what the artist considered to be the label's "factory-like operation methods."[289] As the conflict went on, Wonder employed the ultimate, most drastic tactic of resistance, by simply allowing his standing contract to expire on his 21st birthday in 1971. Gordy eventually agreed to Wonder's demand for increased control over his own projects, and a greater degree of artistic independence, the same compromise he would reach with Marvin Gaye.

Chapter 3: Career Control

"You can't base your life on other people's expectations." – Stevie Wonder

Having reached the age of 21, Wonder was now allowed to withdraw funds independently from his trust fund, and immediately set about to establish his own publishing and recording studio, which he named Black Bull Music and Taurus productions, in line with his astrological sign. In the same year, still estranged from Motown and Gordy, he undertook a study of music theory at the University of Southern California in Los Angeles, and managed to release the album, "Where I'm Coming From," on his own. This was the 13th of the studio albums, released in 1971, the last of the Motown sessions to be released before Wonder's breakup with the studio, and written entirely by Wonder and Syreeta.

Having successfully fulfilled Motown's formula of pop and soul fusion through the early years, Wonder's musical imagination virtually took off following the stalemate with the studio. In the following months, "he went on to compose far more idiosyncratic music,"[290] with an independence never before enjoyed, and showing the beginnings of distinct, signature elements in the later offerings. In addition, he was able to turn the traditional instrumental configuration on its head with his knowledge of the new electronic instruments put out by Moog and others makers of early synthesizers. Understanding the workings of the studio as few other artists did, he became a pioneer of the new synthesizer age that enrapt both the classical and non-classical genres in the '70s and '80s. And, as "one of the few musicians to make records on which he played virtually all the instruments,"[291] he was able to work entirely without supervision, and bypass much of the hovering authority imposed by studio staff. It has been noted that after being given more free rein in 1972, Wonder began to produce songs with "often buoyant lyrics,"[292] and

---

[288] New World Encyclopedia, Stevie Wonder – www.newworldencyclopedia.org/entry/Stevie-Wonder
[289] New World Encyclopedia, Stevie Wonder
[290] Rolling Stone, Stevie Wonder Biography
[291] Rolling Stone, Stevie Wonder Biography

with a more fully-released artistic personality, he seemed to possess an "uncanny ability to turn any public statement into a metaphysical sermon."[293] Free of the narrow Motown formula, and in control of the inner workings of the studio, Wonder's new musical persona exploded into a generation of innovative releases.

At the age of 21 and now in possession of an independent source of funds and a company over which he exerted ultimate control, Wonder was in a far stronger position to negotiate than he had been striking out on his own. It was still not in his best interests to remain outside the powerful organization of Motown, but neither was it in Gordy's interests to allow such a valuable and heralded artist to escape. By the time the two buried the hatchet and Wonder returned to the good graces of Motown, the two had negotiated a $13 million contract. Wonder had been granted a significantly higher royalty rate, and had become a powerhouse musician backed with vast knowledge, a high degree of public popularity, and a new-found self-confidence. Gordy, better than any other, would have realized this, and the new contract was, in his mind, money well spent. For Wonder, the new creative freedom expressed itself most notably in texts that took on, much like Marvin Gaye's, all manner of controversial issues, including poverty, war, drugs, and politics. Such an example as "You Haven't Done Nothing," written and released as a direct "stab at Richard Nixon," would have been impossible at Motown only a short time before. In those years, and true to Gordy's formula for success, Motown was intended to serve as a studio seeking to fulfill the popular soul music model, rather than going out of its way to risk negative ramifications from political controversy.

The album "Music of My Mind" was released in 1972, and by late in the year, another album was issued, now recognized as a historic piece of music: "Talking Book," the 15th album, released in October. This revolutionary issue contained a top hit in the first single, "Superstition," which embodied some of the most advanced electronic work ever heard on the new instruments that had seldom been employed thus far in the genre. In addition to extremely advanced concepts produced on the synthesizer, "Superstition" displayed the sound of a Hohner clavinet, the use of which was pioneered by Wonder, later using an amplified keyboard with the synthesizer. Among listeners, many were confused by the new instrument, only now being introduced to college classes around the nation as a curiosity, and believed it to be a variant of the harpsichord sound.

In general, beginning with "Music of My Mind," Wonder embarked upon a series of musical and technological explorations devoted to many of his "more exotic musical ideas."[294] Melding together all manner of variations with gospel, rock and roll, jazz, African and Latin rhythms, along with the new audio technology, the works that most ably showed Wonder's sudden growth

[292] Andrew Flory, Review of Craig Werner's "Higher Ground: Stevie Wonder, Aretha Franklin, Curtis Mayfield, and the Rise and Fall of American Soul", in *Notes,* Second Series, Vol. 60 No. 3, p. 753

[293] Andrew Flory, p. 753

[294] Rolling Stone, Stevie Wonder Biography

included "Superwoman, Where Were You When I Needed You," "Happier Than the Morning Sun," and "I Love Every Little Thing About You," from the "Music of My Mind" album.

In the case of "Superstition," composed in the funk genre, the choice came down to Wonder or friend Jeff Beck as to which artist would tackle it. Beck had created the drum beat for "Superstition," but eventually, Wonder was the one who would write and produce it as the lead single for "Talking Book." The song quickly became the #1 soul single in the United States, joining with the immense success enjoyed by a second track, "You are the Sunshine of My Life," the 1973 single which peaked at #1 as well. Released somewhat later in 1973, Wonder would not be the first person to sing it on recording; that honor fell instead to singers James Gilstrap and Lani Groves. Beck, the odd man out for the rights to "Superstition," received another song to record.

Such a series of rapid-fire successes, especially "Talking Book," "brought Stevie out of the mini-slump"[295] that he had experienced in terms of chart rankings for the past year. He then went on another tour with the Rolling Stones, and the live exposure raised the album's profile tremendously in terms of sales. In a continuation of Wonder's exploitation of new technology within the studio, especially the synthesizer, Wonder himself played most of the instrumental tracks, in addition to vocals. "Talking Book" represented a clear "extension and refinement of the work begun"[296] with the earlier effort. Fresh off the success of 1972, Wonder continued his "long collaboration with synthesizer pioneers, Tonto's Expanding Head Band,"[297] and continued to ride the wave of new technology into the next generation of audiences and artists. In a variety of textual themes, the album is an exemplary expression of romantic idealism, with Wonder's voice "gorgeously orchestrated on an infinity of tracks."[298] The distinctive cover art was reviewed as being "one of Motown's handsomest covers, braille and all."[299]

1972 would see the end of Wonder's marriage to Syreeta Wright after 18 months, but professionally, the juggernaut of their collaboration was still rolling, even though her efforts were less essential to his process than they had been two years prior. By 1973, "Innervisions" had been released, and would become Album of the Year. Against all the former guidelines of Motown Studios and its CEO, Wonder came out with nine tracks devoted to drug abuse, ("Too High"), racism ("Living for the City"), and love (the ballad "All in Love is Fair"). He didn't call it done until he had taken one more swipe at Richard Nixon in the political attack song "He's Misstra Know It All." The album garnered more respect from the listenership than it did from many of the major critics, although for most of his efforts, the lyrics took more abuse in the reviews than did the music. A *Rolling Stone* critic, in particular, took a fairly caustic view toward "Innervisions," intimating that "just when Stevie had some momentum going, he went and put

[295] New World Encyclopedia, Stevie Wonder

[296] Super Seventies.com, Innervisions, Stevie Wonder – www.superseventies.com/spwondersteveie1.html

[297] Encyclopaedia Britannica, Stevie Wonder Biography

[298] Super Seventies.com, Innervisions

[299] Super Seventies.com, Innervisions

together a concept album of homogenous music and rather typical lyrics…Stevie has lowered the ceiling, and put a damper on his talents."[300] Wonder was, however, again honored at the Grammys that year, and at the award ceremony for Best Album, he refused to take the stage or accept the award unless his mother was permitted to join him at the podium, considering their close collaboration and strong family bonds. He asserted on that night that "her strength has led us to this place."[301]

By that year, Wonder had become the first blind recipient of an Academy Award for the song "I Just Called to Say I Love You." The 1973 American Music Award for Favorite Soul R&B artist was the first of many such honors, and he was nominated for Favorite Pop and Rock Male Artist as well. Wonder's rate of hit releases, and his trajectory of artistic quality, continued to run unhindered until August of 1973, when his world nearly came to an end following a concert appearance in Greenville, South Carolina, at the age of 23. Traveling on a North Carolina highway outside of Durham, Wonder sat in the passenger seat of a 1948 Dodge flatbed truck, asleep with the headphones over his ears, as was so often the case. The driver, friend John Harris, for reasons unknown, became distracted and struck the truck in front when it applied its brakes suddenly. The truck was carrying a massive cargo of logs. As Lulu Mae Hardaway describes it in a set of memoirs, entitled, *Blind Faith: The Miraculous Journey of Lulu Mae Hardaway,* "there was a great grinding of screeches as metal hit metal…one of the great logs disencumbered itself of the truck and came crashing through the windshield, spearing Stevie square in the forehead."[302] Wonder, who also lost his sense of smell and bears several scars from the accident, lay in a coma for several days, and his survival was, for a time, in serious doubt.

The recovery from such a serious accident took up much of the following year, with lingering headaches, other maladies, and a steady diet of medication following after. Wonder's recuperation, however, was deemed successful, and he was cleared for a return to work by the beginning of 1974, at which time he released "First Finale," which took the #1 spot. At this time, he already had another song enjoying success at the top of the charts. In the same year, he not only collaborated with his former wife Syreeta but wrote every note of the music, produced every song, and personally presented her to the public on the record jacket on the album, "Stevie Wonder Presents Syreeta."[303] Around the same time, he was presented with a 1974 American Music Award for Favorite Soul R&B Male Artist for "Innervisions."

To produce such a number of hit albums in the 1970s as a soul artist was both unusual and laudable, as the genre, along with rock 'n' roll, had not truly entered the era in which albums were in the forefront of record sales. For the artists at Motown, it could be easily said that "along with Marvin Gaye and Isaac Hayes, Wonder brought R&B into the album age."[304]

[300] Super Seventies.com, Innervisions

[301] Find A Grave, Lulu Mae Hardaway – www.findagrave.com/cgi-bin/fg.cgi?page=gr&GRid=15188898

[302] IMDb, Steve Wonder Biography – www.imdb.com/name/nm0005567/bio

[303] New World Encyclopedia, Stevie Wonder Biography

[304] Google Play, Stevie Wonder, about the artist – www.play.google.com/store/music/artist/Stevie-Wonder?id=Auywsulg5ftkx2qqc4fplp4m

For Wonder, successful releases were only one of many peripheral changes that overtook the music industry, in part under his direct influence. At the center of the most crucial musical components and social elements of lyrics writing, he brought a fully mature, "peerless melodic facility, [and a] gift for complex arrangements"[305] to bear on the most intricate works in the industry, strongly influenced (as would be the entire subsequent generation of Motown artists) by Marvin Gaye's "What's Going On," a milestone work that signaled a momentous shift in Motown's willingness to address difficult social conflicts.

With the guidelines suddenly loosened within Motown, and having by his mid-20s "mastered virtually every idiom of African-American popular music,"[306] Wonder reached a level of sophistication never before seen in terms of melodic and vocal phrasing in non-classical music, "reminiscent of the greatest jazz singers."[307] Amidst a generation of suave Motown vocalists, Wonder offered an unusual visual, tonal, and personal sense of live stage performance. The "depth and honesty of his emotional projection came straight from the black church music of his childhood,"[308] wrapped in an almost professorial knowledge of the craft and possessing a naturally charged, ecstatic style of delivery, originating in the faith of his childhood.

Chapter 4: Songs in the Key of Life

"I want to take all the pain that I feel and celebrate and turn it around." – Stevie Wonder

Wonder surrounded himself with a group of major talents in 1976 to create an album of greater proportions than had ever been seen in Motown, even more daring than his own. Entitled "Songs in the Key of Life," the impact of this enormous project has left future listeners rating the album as one of the artist's major lifetime achievements. The finished product, after a period of arduous work, over two years, was a double album, created in an era where the concept of an album was only at that time gaining traction. Motown, despite its willingness to maintain an up-to-date view toward albums as a measure of chart success, nevertheless remained skittish about such a collection, and in fits and starts, cancelled a series of releases before finally letting it go to the public. Several calculated announcements resulted in the work being yanked back on the verge of release, being "haggled over, reworked, expanded and gossiped about."[309] The album contains brief and powerful appearances of several high-profile artists, such as George Benson, Herbie Hancock, Minnie Riperton, Bobbie Humphrey, and Syreeta Wright. As with the album before, however, *Rolling Stone* took exception to several of its features, beginning with the artwork, describing it as "a last-minute amateur effort…hideous and cheap." Similarly, the various aspects of the music tracks were open to condemnation or faint praise – "eclecticism, rich and welcome,

---

[305] Google Play, Stevie Wonder, about the artist

[306] Encyclopaedia Britannica, Stevie Wonder

[307] Encyclopaedia Britannica, Stevie Wonder

[308] Encyclopaedia Britannica, Stevie Wonder

[309] Rolling Stone, Songs in the Key of Life, Stevie Wonder – www.rollingstone.com/music/music/albumreviews/songs-in-the-key-of-life-19761216

[but] the overall effect is haphazard."[310]

Raul Ranz's picture of Benson

For Wonder, attaining approval by critics for lyrics that radiated a generally optimistic nature was difficult in this grittier age, and his idealistic lines took the worst of it. Even in the ode to Wonder's daughter in "Isn't She Lovely," his joy over writing and performing the work itself, and the subject, "overcomes [the] lyrics, [which] aren't clever or particularly intelligent, but at

[310] Rolling Stone, Songs in the Key of Life

their best…instinctive, straightforward, and touchingly severe."[311] Even the bonus material of the EP was tossed aside by Rolling Stone as a "more self-indulgent than generous gesture."[312]

Considering the album's relative popularity, one which increased through the following decade, Motown was all but mandated to provide Wonder with increased latitude and could no longer doubt his winning instincts. "Songs in the Key of Life" was the first double album of any artist to debut in the top spot on the charts, a position it maintained for the following 14 weeks consecutively. Two of the album's singles went on to individual fame: "Isn't She Lovely," the sentimental offering to his daughter, and in a more subdued frame of mind, "Village Ghetto Land." Rolling Stone listed the album at number 55 among the publication's 500 greatest of all time.

"Songs in the Key of Life," the 18th album, was considered in the beginning by many other than the critics to be somewhat "difficult to fathom…hard for some listeners to assimilate."[313] This was true, in part, because in his voracious interest in the new technology, and in his increasingly vast understanding of advanced harmony, daring chord extensions and changes, Wonder seemed to out-run his audience for a short while. Some have described this phase of Wonder's career as its "classical period," although such a term does not adequately reference the intense period of innovation. Recorded at Crystal Sound Studios in Hollywood, "Songs in the Key of Life" was written at a time in which Wonder harbored a particular ire for the federal government, and the tracks show it overtly. Occupying the 8th Best Album for the year upon its release four years later, the original working title was "I Ain't Gonna Stand For It." Only the tender "Isn't She Lovely" serves to cool the emotional temperature of the album, a song written several years before the others and a personal favorite that would go on to find a niche as a national institution for weddings, debutante presentations and bat mitzvahs. Furthermore, much of the year was taken up with the establishment and funding of a Home for Blind and Retarded Children as well, the fulfillment of a long-held dream.

More success followed with songs such as "Sir Duke," a musical tribute to the great Duke Ellington. Such a musical salute was fitting, as Wonder, like Ellington, developed such an extensive knowledge of harmony as to stand alone in structural sophistication. Ellington, however, spilled over into classical music idioms, including intricate orchestrations with his extensive harmonic gifts, going in the general direction that Gershwin had gone, where Wonder applied it directly to variants of soul, blues and rock, choosing to raise the bar within his home genres of the non-classical canon, rather than move to one where such practices were more the norm. Winning Grammys almost at will in the decade of the 70s, Paul Simon facetiously addressed the phenomenon in his own 1976 acceptance speech, thanking Wonder profusely before the public for not releasing an eligible album in the previous year. By 1977, "Songs in the

---

[311] Rolling Stone, Songs in the Key of Life
[312] Rolling Stone Songs in the Key of Life
[313] New World Encyclopedia, Stevie Wonder Biography

Key of Life" had become the second best-selling album behind Fleetwood Mac's "Rumours."

Duke Ellington

The soundtrack album, "Hotter Than July," was released in 1979, containing a birthday message for the late Martin Luther King, and Wonder eventually became one of the most high-profile activists that finally succeeded in procuring a national holiday to be celebrated annually in the civil rights leader's name. 1979 also saw the release of "Boogie on a Reggae Woman," the '74 funk single from the album, "Fulfillingness' First Finale." The song was pure funk, not reggae (as is commonly thought), and featured Wonder on harmonica.

Another soundtrack for an unreleased film came out in the same year, entitled "Journey through the Secret Life of Plants," a project that had been three years in the making. The soundtrack was released under the same title, featuring mostly instrumental tracks. Without the customary vocals, the album "failed to catch on,"[314] but the unorthodox instrumentals for the time did, however, serve as a precursor to the tide of New Age music that swept the country soon after.

Chapter 5: The '80s

"You know, I always when people ask me, like, what is my most favorite song, I quote Duke Ellington, when they would ask him, what's his favorite composition? And I say, I haven't written it yet. Because, you know, there are different songs for different occasions." – Stevie Wonder

Most critics and historians cite the late '70s and the early years of the '80s as the zenith of Wonder's career, and specifically point to the end of the former decade as a distinct turning point in his development. Despite touring extensively through much of the '80s, he spent less time in the recording studio than he ever had in previous years, and seemed to put out a smaller trove of ideas upon which to base albums that at one time would have all but guaranteed hit singles. In all of his varied travels, Wonder became the first artist of Motown to visit the Eastern bloc of nations, finding new and appreciative audiences there. However, whether artistic trends of the day passed him by (or vice-versa), or whether, as some critics say, some of his '80s recordings "became sporadic and often lacked focus,"[315] something in the public atmosphere, reinforced by the parallel comments from high level critics, seemingly turned against the one-time "sure thing," all at once. Some are of the opinion that as his passions for specific social issues began to overrun his sense of what would achieve popularity, an undisciplined over-emotionality began to creep into everything Wonder wrote and performed, and that the entire catalogue had become "marred by excesses of sentimentality and less of the progressive imagination of his best work."[316]

As an independent and highly self-directed artist, such critical responses certainly did not dampen Wonder's will to continue, and in 1980 he produced a dance hit entitled "Let's Get Serious" for Jermaine Jackson, the only member of the Jackson family who would remain with Motown after he had married a member of Gordy's family. Wonder also wrote "All I Do," the second single from "Hotter Than July," and a highly sentimental ballad, "Lately." Regardless of trends occurring at the time, "Hotter Than July" went on to become Wonder's first platinum single album.

In 1982, Wonder's friend, Dizzy Gillespie, played the trumpet solo on "Do I Do" from the "Musiquarium" compilation, an interesting choice because, as was the case during Marvin Gaye's collaboration with the great trumpeter, Berry Gordy had considered Gillespie a relic of a former age and had discouraged his artists from imitating his style. In the same year, Wonder teamed up with former Beatle Paul McCartney for another number one single, "Ebony and Ivory," and with Bob Dylan and Jackson Browne for the "Peace Sunday" concert, an anti-nuclear

---

[314] Rolling Stones, Stevie Wonder Biography
[315] Encyclopaedia Brittanica, Stevie Wonder
[316] MSN Entertainment, Stevie Wonder, Biography – www.msn.com/music/artist-biography/stevie-wonder/

event staged at the Rose Bowl in Pasadena. The following year, Wonder was inducted into the Songwriters Hall of Fame. He went on to win the Songwriters Hall of Fame Award in 1983, and set off in 1984 with a harmonica appearance in Chaka Kan's hit "I Feel For You."

Roland Godefroy's picture of Dizzy Gillespie

Quite appropriately, since he was a reigning member of Detroit's most famous music studio, Wonder was once presented the key to the city and actually gave serious consideration to running for the office of mayor, a campaign which did not ultimately move forward. Using his most recent Oscar Award appearance as a forum against the condition of apartheid, Wonder caused great offense to the South African media, as apartheid had not yet been overthrown there. Wonder's music was entirely and abruptly banned from the airwaves. All broadcast media in the South Africa was controlled by the South African Broadcasting Corporation, and the insult taken by Wonder's Oscar night appearance was felt at a national level. Wonder was honored for his work on the song "I Just Called to Say I Love You" in the film "The Woman in Red," but he accepted the award "in the name of Nelson Mandela,"[317] who was at the time serving a life sentence for revolutionary acts against the current government. Wonder's overtly anti-apartheid song, "It's Wrong," made consistently repeated use of the words "wrong" and "hold on tight." The effects of the ban in South Africa, however, actually heightened listeners' views of the work,

[317] The New York Times, Stevie Wonder Music Banned in South Africa – www.nytimes.com/1985/03/27/arts/stevie-wonder-music-banned-in-South-Africa.html

and of Wonder himself, so he suffered no ill effect. In fact, with numerous colleagues within the industry, he participated in the universal hit recorded in the same year, "We are the World," written in a cooperative venture on behalf of the USA for Africa organization.

1985 also saw the release of the LP album "Square Circle," which featured the single "Part-Time Lover." This studio album, Wonder's 20th overall, went on to win a Grammy at the 28th annual awards ceremony. Wonder took over almost every facet of the recording, laying down all the vocals, providing his own sound effects, and playing 13 instruments. "Square Circle" took Wonder over five years to create, but it would eventually go to platinum for his efforts, as would its best single. Numerous other projects occupied his attentions for the year, including a Golden Globe Award and the Afghanistan World Foundation Award. Taking an enormous step out of the Motown tradition, Wonder even played the harmonica alongside Barbara Streisand on "Can't Help Loving That Man of Mine," which appeared on her legendary Broadway album. To end the year, he was nominated for a BAFTA film award for his work on "The Woman in Red."

A 1986 appearance on *The Bill Cosby Show* gave Wonder a chance to truly demonstrate some of the features of the still relatively new synthesizer. In one of the most memorable episodes of the popular series, Wonder gave the audience and cast a "lesson in sampling,"[318] with actress Felicia Rashad singing along. In addition, he participated in the chart-topping "That's What Friends Are For," joining with Gladys Knight, Dionne Warwick, and Elton John, with all the proceeds being donated to AIDS research.

Wonder's high-level collaborations continued in 1987 in a duet with good friend Michael Jackson on the single "Just Good Friends," which appeared on Jackson's "Bad" album. Jackson returned the favor by appearing in Wonder's new 1987 album, "Characters," the final release for Wonder that decade. The album became best known for its single, "Skeletons," and it featured two notable duets, the first with Jackson on "Get It" and the second with Julio Iglesias on "My Love." In 1989, Wonder was inducted into the Rock & Roll Hall of Fame, and played drums for the BBC Hall of Fame.

---

[318] Lisa Respers, CNN Entertainment, Cosby Show: Our 10 Favorite Moments, September 24, 2014

Zoran Veselinovic's picture of Michael Jackson in 1988

Chapter 6: The '90s

Alan Light's picture of Stevie Wonder at a rehearsal for the Grammy Awards in 1990

"I can't say that I'm always writing in my head but I do spend a lot of time in my head writing or coming up with ideas. And what I do usually is write the music and melody and then, you know, maybe the basic idea. But when I feel that I don't have a song or just say, God, please give me another song. And I just am quiet and it happens." – Stevie Wonder

A new collaboration in 1991 seemed to rejuvenate Wonder and his musical imagination when he teamed with legendary filmmaker Spike Lee in the film "Jungle Fever." Singles from the soundtrack album included "Gotta Have You," "Feeding Off the Love of the Land," and "These Three Words." The old flair and creative process sprang back into the all-new material for "Natural Wonder" and "Conversation Peace," and with these two projects, the critics began to back away from their relentless assaults on Wonder's work during the '80s. One critic wrote that "it was Stevie back in vintage form; beautiful catchy melodies intermixed with meaningful lyrics and funky rhythms."[319]

In the following two years, Wonder was honored as the recipient of the Nelson Mandela Award and was also awarded an ASCAP Film and Television Music Award for "Jungle Fever."

---

[319] History of Rock, Stevie Wonder – www.history-of-rock.com/stevie-wonder.htm

He also performed "Blowin' in the Wind" for Bob Dylan's 30th anniversary tribute, held at the Rock & Roll Hall of Fame Inductions.

In 1995, "Conversation Peace" became Wonder's 25th album, and he achieved some indirect notoriety when rapper Coolio "put a rap spin"[320] on "Pastime, Paradise," which he retitled "Gangsta's Paradise." Despite well-liked singles such as "Tomorrow Robins Will Sing," and "For Your Love," "Conversation Peace" was one of Wonder's few "commercial disappointment[s]."[321] Critic Robert Christgau offered telling comments about Wonder's flirtation with every performer's fear of becoming old news, a nostalgia artist, relenting somewhat to remind the reader that although everything on the 2nd album had been heard before in various parts of Wonder's past work, it had still, fortunately, not entirely worn out its welcome.

After years of increasing respect as a centerpiece to Wonder's professional life, "A Song in the Key of Life," the 18th album, became the subject of a documentary film, and the musicians who had contributed to the epic double album gathered for a reunion. That same year, 1996, Wonder appeared at the closing ceremonies for the Atlanta Summer Olympic Games, and at a charity event that year, he was able to fulfill a fond wish that had eluded him throughout his adult life: driving a car. He was invited, and coached, to drive James Bond's BMW Roadster onto the stage from the wings. He was also presented with an honorary doctorate from the University of Alabama in Birmingham.

In a serious 1997 collaboration that brought a distasteful issue back to the forefront of Wonder's efforts, he participated in a duet with Babyface on the single, "How Come, How Long," a sharp commentary on domestic abuse from Babyface's album "The Day." Inspired by the grisly Nicole Brown Simpson case, the album was nominated twice for a Grammy. Wonder received partial praise for "Gangsta's Paradise" with an ASCAP Film and Television Music Award, and was similarly honored at that year's MTV Video Music Awards.

At the age of 49, Stevie Wonder became the youngest recipient in the 22 year history of the Kennedy Center Honors when he received one of the Lifetime Achievement Awards from then president Bill Clinton. An interesting project took place in the same year, with Wonder recording a purely instrumental jazz album under the name of Eivets Rednow (Stevie Wonder spelled backwards). It was an odd assortment of tracks sewn together from unwanted takes stashed away for years in the studio, and Wonder and Gordy could not have been truly surprised that the quirky and excessive exercise did not attract a particularly enthused response; if anything, it's a surprise to many that the unpredictable head of Motown let the album out at all.

---

[320] Stevie Wonder Biography – www.stevie-wonder.net/bio.htm
[321] MSN Entertainment: Stevie Wonder

Chapter 7: Recent Years

"I am what I am. I love me! And I don't mean that egotistically - I love that God has allowed me to take whatever it was that I had and to make something out of it." – Stevie Wonder

At the start of a new decade, Wonder collaborated with Spike Lee once again by contributing two soundtrack albums for the 2000 film "Bamboozled": "Misrepresented People" and "Some Years Ago." Lee's film fell under a largely undefined category of "black satire" and smacked of the old stereotype of "minstrelsy," with a story based on black performers wearing black-face. Also in 2000, Wonder received an ASCAP Film and Television Music Award for "Wild, Wild West," starring Will Smith. Before the end of the year, he had also won the unwanted "Razzie" Award for the title song bearing the same name as the film's title.

2001 was not such a good one for Wonder, as he experienced multiple legal difficulties with several women he had been involved with during his earlier days. In 2001, he married Kai Milla Morris, but he was sued by a former wardrobe assistant, Angela McAfee, who claimed that she had contracted genital herpes from Wonder over the course of their five-year affair. Despite never being married to Wonder, McAfee's suit was based on palimony, and she alleged that he [Wonder] "pursued her for more than a decade…ultimately persuaded her…to quit working as a wardrobe consultant and move into his Los Angeles estate."[322] McAfee further alleged that the two had made a verbal agreement that he would be the only breadwinner in the family, and she further asserted that she had redesigned his estate with a Braille system, prepared dietary and exercise regimens intended to lower his cholesterol rate and generally promote his good health, and that once she had done these things, he abruptly moved out of the house and stopped paying rent, as if she had never existed. Wonder, on the other hand, claimed that McAfee had stolen over $160,000 of valuable property from him. With the matter in court for an extended period of time, a judge sought to end the conflict after a year by pressuring them to settle out of court.

Wonder had also met Yolanda Simmons when she applied to his publishing company as a secretary, and although they never married, they had three children together: Aisha Morris, Keita Morris, and Kwame Morris. With Melody McCulley, who had worked with Wonder as a backup, he had Emkow Mumtaz Morris, later a budding R&B singer, and Sophia Morris. His last two children were named Kailand Morris and Mandla Kadjay Carl Stevan Morris, born to Kai Milla Morris. Kailand appeared with his father as a drummer on one occasion, but Kai and Wonder would separate eight years after being married in 2001. She would go on to establish a line of luxury fashion clothing, and Michelle Obama and actress Eva Mendes became regular clients.

Wonder's seemingly facetious remark, "I do believe in women – I really do," perhaps satirically based on the Tin Man's iconic line from "The Wizard of Oz," seems a flippant expression of a difficult truth for not only Wonder but for many of those who reach stardom in

---

[322] NNDB, Stevie Wonder – www.nndb.com/people/535/000022469/

his industry. The state of his later relationships with former wives and partners is unknown, but Wonder reportedly maintains good relationships with his children.

Wonder had a special fondness for the great reggae artist Bob Marley, and in 2001, he found the opportunity to work with Marley's sons Damian and Steven. Within the following months, he performed for the opening ceremonies of the Winter Paralympics in Salt Lake City, won the George and Ira Gershwin Lifetime Achievement Award at UCLA'S "Spring Sing," and received the Sammy Cahn Lifetime Achievement Award from the Songwriters Hall of Fame in 2002.

The remainder of the decade would be spent in sporadic, individual performances and projects, with a mixture of professional success and personal gain and loss. In 2004, Billboard placed Wonder 15th on the Rolling Stone list of the 100 Greatest Rock & Roll Artists of All Time, but in the same year, Syreeta died of breast cancer. He received the Billboard Century Award and the Johnny Mercer Award, and witnessed the birth of two children, Mandla Kadjay and Carl Stevan Morris, the last of seven. With his rate of musical production slowing considerably, "A Time to Love" was written and finally released after a 10 year hiatus.

2005 brought Wonder's first album release, "A Time to Love," in a decade. On the highlight of the album, he was joined by daughter Aisha for the single "From the Bottom of My Heart," an effort that won him the Best Male Pop Vocal Performance at the 48th Annual Grammys. Also included was the single "What's the Fuss," featuring Prince on guitar. "A Time to Love" was the title single of the album and addressed the social and political thrust of the album: "We have time for racism, we have time for criticism, held bondage by our ism's, when will there be a time to love." Soon after, he performed in the all-star Live 8 Concert in Philadelphia, part of a simultaneous string of concerts held simultaneously around the world that involved over a thousand musicians and was widely broadcast around the world. In a nod to how highly he's regarded, Wonder was asked to close the show.

The early years of the new century brought many one-time collaborations and unusual appearances, but the stream of album and hit singles Wonder had always maintained came to an end. In 2006, he performed for the pre-game at Super Bowl XL and sang with his four-year old son accompanying on drums. Wonder also accompanied Aretha Franklin for the national anthem. Despite not being ordinarily fond of television, he became a mentor for an installment of American Idol, but the young singers found the songs surprisingly virtuosic and vocally difficult to handle. Most agree that due to his understanding of advanced harmony and melisma (the use of multiple notes, sometimes sung very rapidly), Wonder's songs are "renowned for being difficult to sing…[he had] a highly developed sense of harmony, using many extended chords…his melodies often make abrupt, unpredictable changes, and include melismatic vocalizations."[323] Not sticking to the comfortable keys and arpeggio patterns of pop music, he ventured into key centers "more often found in jazz,"[324] such as the generally problematic e flat

---

[323] New World Encyclopedia, Stevie Wonder

minor, and others generally problematic for vocalists and keyboard players who have not taken a thorough study of music theory. A few of the less experienced "Idol" singers were not able to follow the songs' structural paths or imitate virtuoso vocal abilities displayed by Wonder on his own songs.

In 2006, Wonder performed for the Washington, D.C. celebration, "A Capitol Fourth," shortly after the loss of his beloved mother, Lulu Mae Hardaway. Touring seemed to serve as a natural salve for Wonder, and he had always seemed to relish it. Thus, in 2007, he announced a "Wonder's Summer Night" tour, to consist of 13 concerts and an itinerary that would take him to far-flung locations in the U.S., Europe, the U.K., Australia, and New Zealand. It would be his first real tour in over a decade.

As a self-described "liberal democrat," Wonder was active in the presidential campaign to help elect Barack Obama. He was outspoken against foreign military intervention, on the part of the United States in particular, and during 2008, he wrote the tribute for Mariah Carey's endorsement in *Time* magazine's "100 Most Influential People in the World." Voted the 9th greatest singer of the rock era by *Rolling Stone*, he received a star on the Hollywood Walk of Fame and was nominated for an NAACP Award.

2009 was yet another year of more accolades and losses. Appointed as a United Nations Messenger of Peace in February, Wonder also received the Gershwin Prize for Pop Music from President Obama. It was only the second time that the prize has been presented, and his visit to the White House resulted in a concert performed in the East Room. Wonder also performed with the Jonas brothers on "Superstition" at the 51st Grammy Awards, and he became the fourth artist ever to receive the Montreux Jazz Festival Spirit Award. On the other hand, Wonder, along with many others in the industry and around the world, was stunned by the death of friend Michael Jackson, with whom he had enjoyed excellent collaborations. Attending the memorial service, Wonder sang "Never Dreamed You'd Leave in Summer."

[324] New World Encyclopedia, Stevie Wonder

A picture of Stevie Wonder being given the Gershwin Award by President Obama

Continuing into the current decade, Wonder has come across more like an emeritus of music than as an ongoing participant. He is now more likely to make headlines by putting in an occasional appearance for a one-time event or accepting the occasional award, but on rare occasions, he still puts together a musical release or tour, albeit ones that are less ambitious than the great ones from previous decades. In 2010, he was nominated for induction into the New Jersey Hall of Fame, and he was inducted into the Apollo Legends Hall of Fame in 2011. He also put in a surprise appearance at a national Martin Luther King celebration.

Winning the Billboard Music Icon Award in 2012, Wonder opened himself up to rare personal criticism with his comments about actor and R&B singer Frank Ocean's decision to come out. At the time, stars who came out interested the industry, and Ocean had written for several popular performers, including Justin Bieber, John Legend, and Béyonce. Wonder suggested that among the gay population, some people who believe themselves to be gay are actually confused, and not gay at all. He added the comment that "people can mistake closeness for love."[325] The comments were taken as an anti-gay statement, for which he apologized publicly soon after, having never

---

[325] Huffpost, Gay Voices, Stevie Wonder, Frank Ocean: Some People Who Think They're Gay, They're Confused – www.huffingtonpost.com/2012/08/31/stevie-wonder-frank-ocean-gaycomment-_n_1846928.html

intended to insult the gay community, and reminding the public that he had, as much as any other, always supported love in any personal and social form. As he once put it, "Clearly, love is love, between a man and a woman, a woman and a man, a woman and a woman and a man and a man."

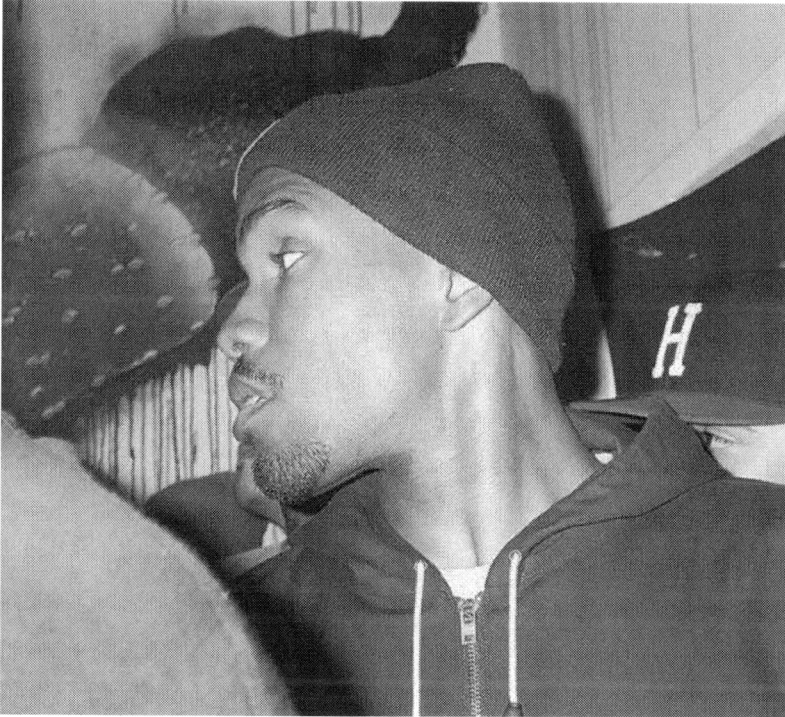

Dave Gold's picture of Frank Ocean

Personal convictions on social issues again came to the forefront in 2013. Among the headlines in the music industry was Wonder's announcement that he would perform a concert in Marrakesh, June 28, 2013, if international negotiators would make good on their earlier promise to form an international treaty that would "provide blind and visually impaired individuals worldwide with more access to books." On June 27, a United Nations-backed forum that included over 600 such negotiators and represented 186 nations accomplished the task. Following the acquittal of George Zimmerman in the shooting death of Trayvon Martin, Wonder announced that he would initiate a boycott against the state of Florida in every way he could, including concert appearances, until the controversial "stand your ground" law was eliminated from the state books.

Fulfilling an earlier promise to his mother, Wonder also began work on a gospel album dedicated to her, including, he speculated beforehand, at least one song to be performed in Arabic. Simultaneous with his work on the gospel album ("Ten Billion Hearts"), he worked on a second effort, "When the World Began." Both were targeted for release in 2014. Along with the release of "When the World Began," was an announcement that Wonder would "return to Brazil for the third time to perform in Brasilia…and San Paulo."[326]

Antonio Cruz's picture of Stevie Wonder for Agência Brasil.

In conjunction with those efforts, 2014 saw an uptick in artistic creativity for Wonder, as one of his songs, "Another Star," was chosen by the BBC as the theme for covering the World Cup in Brazil. He announced plans to join Aerosmith at the Clapham Festival in London as a headliner, and it was rumored that he would release two more albums over the following year. Having already been presented with the Spirit Award for the Montreux Jazz Festival, he agreed to appear as a performer at the event for the first time; the founder of the festival, Claude Nobs, had attempted to book Wonder many times, but simply "couldn't afford him."[327] Sadly, the two were never to meet because Nobs was killed in a 2013 skiing accident in Europe, but in 2014, Wonder

---

[326] DTG Reviews, Stevie Wonder to drop When the World Began/Ten Billion Hearts in 2014 – www.dtgre.com/2013/2013/11/stevie-wonder-to-drop-when-the-world.html

[327] Contact Music, Stevie Wonder to pay gospel tribute to his mother, 26 June, 2013 – www.contactmusic.com/news/stevie-wonder-to-pay-gospel-tribute-to-his-mother_3735209

appeared in the 48th edition of the festival and singled out producer Quincy Jones from the audience in tribute. He received an ASCAP Centennial Award with fellow musicians Billy Joel, Garth Brooks, Joan Baez, and Stephen Sondheim to celebrate the 100th anniversary of the organization and to celebrate and promote its first fundraiser.

Rumors of an album scheduled to be released in 2015 abounded again throughout the industry, and one source close to the action spoke of an unusually high degree of secrecy within Wonder's immediate circle: "It's still in the early stages – he's got security on the doors to ensure no one hears a whisper."[328] Touring was, as always, a buzzword in the latest rumors, certainly the natural course of action to take in order to promote a new release, but arrangements for such a tour are still unclear.

Wonder once said, "I am all for anything that is going to better equip a person who is physically challenged in any way, to have an opportunity to be able to do what they are able to do," and it was reported by some that he has recently expressed an interest in what has been referred to as the "Geordi La Forge"[329] surgery. The surgery is a reference to a prominent Star Trek character who compensates for lack of sight with a visor through which he can sense shape, color and movement. Medically, it is uncertain whether such a surgery would truly provide viable eyesight, and Wonder has remarked more than once along the way that he "would probably not last a minute if I were able to see things."[330] Either way, Wonder has not undergone such a surgery to date.

Regardless of his slowed rate of creative releases, or the status of those ideas and goals still unrealized in the studio or on the stage, it is clear that Stevie Wonder "remains a potent, if intermittent, force on the recording and performing fronts."[331] His mere presence in the business has exerted a tremendous influence over colleagues, in the United States and overseas, from the likes of George Benson to Bob Marley. In the course of a career stretching through five decades, he has collaborated with artists such as B.B. King, the Jacksons, The Supremes, Minnie Riperton, Rufus, and Elton John, who has remarked that wherever he travels, a copy of "Songs in the Key of Life" goes with him. Steeped in the atmosphere of black church music, even Wonder's latest creations carry a tinge of the heightened shiver with which authentic gospel can fill a room; listeners could say that Wonder's music is generally secular but always carries a sense of gospel rhetoric, and that in keeping with art grounded in faith, he emits a general sense of optimism in everything he writes, records, performs, and releases.

Wonder has taken on many of the world's woes, using his talents to heighten global AIDS awareness, to spur the hastening of apartheid's end, to address the ever-present dangers of drunk driving and drug abuse in his home country through his support of MADD, and to relentlessly

[328] Media Mass, Stevie Wonder New Studio Album and Tour in 2015? – www.en.mediamass.net/people/stevie-wonder/new-album.html
[329] NNDB, Stevie Wonder – www.nndb.com/people535/000022469/
[330] IMDb, Stevie Wonder Biography
[331] Rock & Roll Hall of Fame, Stevie Wonder Biography

fund-raise for those who cannot generate the necessary support, the disabled and homeless. When he addressed the issues of violence in America, both domestic and on the street in the 1980s, Wonder himself had the unsettling sense that he was fighting an unusually uphill battle in this new era, as other music genres were, at the same time, "espous[ing] the virtues of street violence and [the] disrespecting of one's fellow man…and more particularly, woman."[332] The undercurrent of texts near the end of the 80s more frequently and graphically probed the underbelly of society's woes while Wonder's customary optimism began to lack the edge of controversy so sought-after by the listening public.

Wonder has announced plans to begin yet another tour of 10 cities in November 2014, beginning with New York City and featuring highlights from the album of the '70s, "Songs in the Key of Life." The tour is a reaction against recent events in the news, in particular the shooting of an unarmed black citizen by police in Ferguson, Missouri. Additional music featured on the tour will include up 40-50 new songs, written in recent years, in preparation for the release of a new album in 2015, "Through the Eyes of Wonder." The artist claims that these songs, and the tour itself, is "partly inspired by monitoring world news,"[333] and by Wonder's intention to react musically to everything negative that he can, suggesting that we have entered an age where we are "living in a time of disposable love."[334] Such domestic events, and ongoing tragedies in the Middle East, seem to have reawakened old energies in Wonder's ability to create prolifically. Likewise, he has retained his youthful energy for hard work in the studio and outside of it, even at the age of 65. The tour's itinerary ends in Oakland, California in December, with several of the singles from the upcoming album scheduled for release by February 2015.

From his days as Motown's "Golden Child"[335] through the next several decades, Stevie Wonder amassed an almost unparalleled list of achievements, and any who came close to statistically matching him in later years did so by riding the wave of his inspiration. In all, he wrote, produced, played, sang and orchestrated twenty-three studio albums, three soundtrack recordings, four live albums, eleven compilations, one box set, a double album, and almost one hundred singles, a great many of them high-ranking hits. As for the charts and sales, the center of Motown's measuring stick, twelve of Wonder's albums reached the top ten, along with more than thirty singles, a full third of his singles output. To date, album sales have topped 150 million units, and he has been awarded 26 Grammy awards, among countless other honors given to him by diverse arts organizations. Further, amidst such a list of professional accomplishments and personal efforts directed toward the enlightening of society through music, it must be noted that Stevie Wonder's career may yet be far from finished, with new releases and tours in the works, ongoing collaborations to be fulfilled, with a new generation of stars from Motown and the larger musical world.

---

[332] Classic Motown, Motown Artist: Stevie Wonder – www.classicmotown.com/artist_pages/stevie-wonder/
[333] Ryan Pearson, Yahoo News, Stevie Wonder Challenges Ferguson Mayor, Sept. 11, 2014
[334] Ryan Pearson, Yahoo News
[335] Rock & Roll Hall of Fame, Stevie Wonder Biography

Online Resources

Other books about music by Charles River Editors

Other books about soul music on Amazon

Bibliography

ABKO, Artists, Sam Cooke – www.abko.com/index.php/artists/artist/16/sam-cooke

American Masters, Sam Cooke, Crossing Over – www.pbs.org

Bio.com, Sam Cooke Biography – Singer, Songwriter (1931 – 1954) – www.biography.com/people/sam-cooke-9256129#synopsis

Classic Bands.com, Sam Cooke – www.classicbands.com/cooke.html

Cloud, David W., Adherents.com, Home Page, the Religious Affiliation of Rock and Roll Legend Sam Cooke – www.adherents.com/people/pc/sam-cooke.html

Concord Music Group, Specialty Records – www.concordmusicgroup.com/labels/Specialty/

Dirt City Chronicles, Death by Misadventure, Sam Cooke – www.dirtchronicles.blogspot.com/2012/07/death-by-misadventure-sam-cooke.html

Eder, Bruce, MSN Entertainment, Sam Cooke Biography – www.msn.com/music/artist.biography/sam-cooke/

Elliott, Jimmie, Mississippi Writers and Musicians – www.mswritersandmusicians.com/musicians/sam-cooke/bio/

Encyclopedia.com, Sam Cooke – www.encyclopedia.com/topic/Sam_Cooke.aspx

Ganz, Jacob, NPR Music, The Record, Sam Cooke at 80: The career that could have been, Jan. 21, 2011

Guralnick, Peter, "Dream Boogie: The Triumph of Sam Cooke, Preview of Morris S. Levy", in *Notes,* Music Library Assocation, Vol. 63, No. 1, September 2066

History of Rock, Sam Cooke – www.history-of-rock.com/cooke.htm

IMDb, Sam Cooke Biography – www.imdb.com/name/nm/10774921/bio?ref_=nm_ov_bio_sm

Kirby, Michael, Way Back Attack, Sam Cooke – www.waybackattack.com/cookesam.html

Krajicek, David, Crime Library, the Death of Sam Cooke – www.crimelibrary.com/notorious_murders/celebrity/Sam-Cooke/13.html

Lydia Hutchinson, Performing Songwriter, The Mysterious Death of Sam Cooke – www.performingsongwriter.com/mysterious-death-sam-cooke/

Mississippi Blues Trail, Sam Cooke – www.bluestrail.org/blues-trail-markers/sam-cooke

Nadal, James, All About Jazz, Sam Cooke – www.musicians.allaboutjazz.com/samcooke

Neal, Mark Anthony, Black Voices, Sept. 18, 2014, Remembering Sam Cooke and the Sounds of Young America, Huffington Post – www.huffingtonpost.com/mark-anthony-neal/remembering-sam-cooke-sound-b-2280523.htm

New World Encyclopedia, Sam Cooke – www.newworldencyclopedia.com/entry/Sam-Cooke

NPR Music, NPR STAFF, Feb. 1, 2014, Sam Cooke and the Song That Almost Scared Him – www.npr.org/2014/02/01/268995033/sam-cooke-and-the-song-that-almost-scared-him

Palmer, Robert, "The Pop Life" – New York Times, January 29, 1986

Rare Soul.com, Bobby Womack Marries Sam Cooke's Widow; Gets Pistol-Whipped, 02/24/13

Ritz, David, Encyclopaedia Britannica.com/EBchecked/topic/136091/Sam-Cooke/93148/works

Rock & Roll Hall of Fame, Sam Cooke Biography – www.rockhall.com/inductees/sam-cooke/bio/

Rolling Stone, Happy Belated Birthday to the Great Sam Cooke – www.rollingstone.com/music/news/happy-belated-80th-birthday-to-the-great-sam-cooke

Rolling Stone, Sam Cooke – www.rollingstone.com/music/artists/sam-cooke/biography

Shane, Ken, Pop Dose, TV Review: "Sam Cooke: Crossing Over" – American Masters PBS, Jan. 11, 2010

Shaw Star.com, Sam Cooke Biography – www.shawstar.com/music/sam-cooke.htm

Star Pulse.com, Sam Cooke Biography – www.starpulse.com/music/Cooke_Sam/Biography

Walker, Brittany M., Carl Franklin to Direct New Cooke Biopic – Casting Has Begun, Euroweb – www.euroweb.com/2013/03/carl-franklin-to-direct-sam-cooke-in-biopic-casting-has-begun

Wolff, David, "You Send Me: The Life and Times of Sam Cooke – He Gave Us Water, Review by Darryl Cox", in *The Threepenny Review*, No. 67, Autumn, 1996

Agony Shorthand, Pinetoppers, "Shout Bamalama/Fat Gal" – www.agonyshorthand.com/pinetoppers-shout-bamalama-fat-gal-45.html

Barlow, Jack, "Otis Redding's Widow," in *Salon* – www.salon.com/2013/08/otis-reddings-widow-i-always-thought-that-everything-he-sang-he-sang-for-me

Bello, Christopher, The Harvard Crimson, the Death of Otis Redding, Jan. 11, 1968/1/11/the-death-of-otis-redding-ptho

Bio.Com, Otis Redding Biography – www.biography.com/people/otis-redding-9453430

Bowman, Rob, "The Stax Sound: A Musicological Analysis", in *Popular Music*, Vol. 14 No. 3, Oct. 1995

D'Ambrosio, Brian, Portal Wisconsin.org, "The Day Otis Redding Died, December 10, 1967, Lake Monona, Wisconsin – www.portalwisconsin.wordpress.com/2010/12/06/the-day-otis-redding-dieddecember-10-1967-lakemonona-wi/

De Main, Bill, Performing Songwriter, "Otis Redding's "(Sittin' On) The Dock Of The Bay" – www.performingsongwriter.com/otis-redding-sittin-dock-bay

Encyclopedia.com, Otis Redding – www.encyclopedia.com/topic/Otis_Redding.aspx

English! Info, Carla Thomas – www.englishturkcebilgi.com/Carla+Thomas/

Free Webs.com, Soul in All Areas, Otis Redding – www.freewebs.com/soulinthehind/otisredding.htm

Guralnick, Peter, "Sweet Soul Music: Rhythm and Blues and the Southern Dream of Freedom," Review by Robert Cochran in *The Journal of American Folklore*, Vol. 100 No. 396, April – June, 1987

History of Rock, Otis Redding – www.history-of-rock.com/otis_redding.htm

Lewis, Randy, L.A. Times, Booker T. Resurrects Memphis Sound with "Sound the Alarm" – June 25, 2013

MSN Entertainment, Otis Redding Biography: Soul Ambassador – www.msn.com/music/artist-biography/otis-redding/

Museum of American Soul Music, Otis Redding – www.staxmuseum.com/about/artists/view/otis-redding

News 1, Otis Redding – www.otisredding.com/anything_slides/news-1/

NNDB, Tracking the Entire World, Otis Redding – www.nndb.com/people/00062679

New World Encyclopedia, Otis Redding – www.newworldencyclopedia.org/entry//Otis-Redding

NPR Music, Music Articles "(Sittin' On) The Dock of the Bay – www.npr.org/2009/09/17/1082281/-sittin-on-the-dock-of-the-bay, September 17, 2000

Oldies.com, Otis Redding Biography – www.oldies.com/artist-biography/Otis-Redding.html

Otis Redding Bio 7 – www.oltisredding.com/anything_slides/bio7/

Otis Redding, the King of Soul – www.otisredding.com#&panel1-9

Ritz, David, Encyclopaedia Britannica, Otis Redding – www.britannica.com/EBchecked/topic/494636/Otis-Redding

Ritz, David, "Happy Song: Soul Music in the Ghetto", in *Salmagundi*, No. 12, Spring, 1970, Skidmore College

Rock & Roll Hall of Fame, Otis Redding Biography – www.rockhall.com/inductees/otis-redding/bio

Star Pulse.com, Otis Redding Biography – www.starpulse.com/Music/Redding_Otis/Biography

Starrs, Chris, New Georgia Encyclopedia, Arts & Culture, Otis Redding (1941-1967) – www.georgiaencyclopedia.org/articles/arts-culture/otis-redding-1941-1967

The Guardian, Booker T. Jones – www.theguardian.com/music/2013/sep12/booker-t-jones-sound-alarm-interview

The Telegraph, Otis Redding Obituary – www.legacy.com/obituaries/Macon/obituary.aspx?pid=16154044

Ward, Brian, "Just My Soul Responding: Rhythm and Blues, Black Consciousness, and Race Relations", Review by Clyde Woods in *The Georgia Historical Quarterly*, Vol. 83 No. 4, Winter 1999

World News, Otis Redding Biography – www.wn.com/Otis-Redding

Ankeny, Jason, All Music.com, Artist Blog, Marvin Gaye – www.allmusic.com/artist/marvin-gaye-mn0000316834/biography

Bio.com, Marvin Gaye Biography – www.biography.com/people/marvin-gaye-9307988

Classic Bands.com, Marvin Gaye – www.classicbands.com/gaye.html

Encyclopedia.com, Marvin Gaye – www.encyclopedia.com/topic/Marvin_Gaye.aspx

FAM People.com, Marvin Gaye Biography – www.fampeople.com/cat-marvin-gaye_6

Find a Death.com, Marvin Gaye – www.findadeath.com/Deceased/9/MarvinGaye/marvin_gaye.htm

Guide Chart.com, Marvin Gaye – www.guidechart.com/marvin-gaye-biography.php

IMDb, Marvin Gaye Biography – www.imdb.com/name/nm0310848/nio?ref_=nm_ov_bio

Kiel, Charles, Review of David Ritz's "Divided Soul: The Life of Marvin Gaye", in the *Society for Ethnomusicology*, Vol. 31 no. 2, 1987

Krajicek, David, Crime Library, The Life and Death of Marvin Gaye – www.crimelibrary.com/notorious_murders/celebrity/Marvin_gaye/index.html

Mazama, Anna, Review of Michael Eric Dyson's "Mercy Mercy Me, the Art, Loves and Demons of Marvin Gaye", in *African American Review*, Vol. 40 No. 20

NPR Music, What's Going On: A Departure That Defined a Generation – www.npr.org/2011/06/01/136818199/whats-going-on-defined-a-generation

PBS, American Masters, Marvin Gaye Timeline – www.pbs.org/wnet/americanmasters/episodes/marvin-gaye/career-timeline/74

R&B, Hall of Fame.com, Marvin Gaye

Ritz, David, Marvin Gaye Biography, Sing365.com/lyric.nsf/Marvin-Gaye-Biography/2479E1513170C15348256BD40017645

Ritz, David, PBS, American Masters, Marvin Gaye, "What's Going On" – PBS.org/wnet/americanmasters/episodes/marvin-gaye/whats-going-on/73

Rock & Roll Hall of Fame, Marvin Gaye Biography – www.rockhall.com/inductees/Marvin-Gaye/bio

Rolling Stone Artists, Marvin Gaye Biography – www.rollingstone.com/music/artists/marvin-gaye/biography

Songwriter Universe, "Amazing Saga: the detailed story of how author David Ritz wrote Sexual Healing with Marvin Gaye – www.songwriteruniverse.com/davidritz.html

SOS, Sound on Sound, Marvin Gaye, "What's Going On" – Classical Tracks – www.soundonsound.com/sos/jul11/articles/classic-tracks-0711.htm

Star Pulse.com, Marvin Gaye Biography – www.starpulse.com/music/Marvin_Gaye/Biography

This Day in History, Marvin Gaye's shot and killed by his own father – www.history.com/this-day-in-history/marvin-gaye-is-shot-and-killed-by-his-own-father

Top Documentary Films – "Marvin Gaye: His Final Hours" – www.topdocumentaryfilms.com/marvin-gaye-his-final-hours/

Awkward, Michael. *Soul Covers: Rhythm and Blues Remakes and the Struggle for Artistic Identity*. Durham: Duke University Press, 2007. Print.

Bego, Mark. *Aretha Franklin: The Queen of Soul*. New York: Da Capo Press, 2001. Print.

Christgau, Robert. *Grown Up All Wrong: 75 Great Rock and Pop Artists from Vaudeville to Techno*. Cambridge, MA: Harvard University Press, 1998. Print.

Dobkin, Matt. *I Never Loved a Man the Way I Love You: Aretha Franklin, Respect, and the Making of a Soul Music Masterpiece*. New York: St. Martin's Press, 2006. Print.

Jackson, Buzzy. *A Bad Woman Feeling Good: Blues and the Women Who Sing Them*. New York: W.W. Norton & Company, 2005. Print.

McAvoy, Jim. *Aretha Franklin*. New York: Chelsea House Publishers, 2002. Print.

Prial, Dunstan. *The Producer: John Hammond and the Soul of American Music*. New York: Farrar, Straus and Giroux, 2006. Print.

Ritz, David. *Respect: The Life of Aretha Franklin*. New York: Hachette Book Group, 2014. E-Book.

Werner, Craig. *Higher Ground: Stevie Wonder, Aretha Franklin, Curtis Mayfield, and the Rise and Fall of American Soul*. New York: Crown Publishing Group, 2007. E-Book.

Winkler, Peter. "Writing Ghost Notes: The Poetics and Politics of Transcription." In

Keeping Score: Music, Disciplinarity, Culture. Eds. David Schwartz, et al. Charlottesville: University of Virginia Press, 1997. Print.

Zeisler, Andy. *Feminism and Pop Culture*. Berkeley: Seal Press, 2008. Print.

Bio.Com, Stevie Wonder Biography – www.biography.com/people/stevie-wonder-9536078#synopsis

Contact Music; Stevie Wonder to pay gospel tribute to his mother – 26 June, 2013 – www.contactmusic.com/news/stevie-wonder-to-pay-gospel-tribute-to-his-mother_3735209

Classic Motown, Motown Artist: Stevie Wonder – www.classicmotown.com/artist_pages/stevie-wonder/

DTG Reviews, Ten Billion Hearts in 2013 – www.dtgre.com/2013/2013/11/stevie-wonder-to-drop-when-world.html

Encyclopaedia Britannica, Stevie Wonder – www.britannica.com/EBchecked/topics/647209/Stevie-Wonder

Find a Grave, Lulu Mae Hardaway – www.findagrave.com/cgi-bin/fg.cgi?page=gr&GRid-15188898

Flory, Andrew, Review of Craig Werner's "Higher Ground: Stevie Wonder, Aretha Franklin. Curtis Mayfield, and the Rise and Fall of American Soul", in Notes, Second Series, Vol. 16, No. 3

Google Play, Stevie Wonder, about the artist – www.play.google.com/store/music/artist/Stevie_Wonder?id=Auywsulg5ftkx2qqc4fplp4m

History of Rock, Stevie Wonder – www.historyofrock.com/stevie_wonder.htm

Huffington Post, Gay Voices, Stevie Wonder, Frank Ocean: Some People Who Think They're Gay, They're Confused – www.huffingtonpost.com/2012/08/31/stevie-wonder-frank-ocean-haycomment-_n_1846928.html

Media Mass, Stevie Wonder, New Studio Album and Tour in 2015? – www.en.mediamass.net/people/stevie-wonder/new-album.htm

MSN Entertainment, Stevie Wonder: Biography – www.msn.com/music/artist-biography/stevie-wonder

New World Encyclopedia, Stevie Wonder – www.newworldencyclopedia.org/entry/Stevie_Wonder

NNDB, Stevie Wonder – www.nndb.com/people/535/00002469/

Pearson, Ryan, Yahoo News, Stevie Wonder Challenges Ferguson Mayor, Sept. 11, 2014

Respers, Lisa, CNN Entertainment, Cosby Show: Our 10 Favorite Moments – www.cnn.com/2014/09/19/showbiz/tv/cosby-show-moments-index.html

Reuters.com, Stevie Wonder Blends Hits at Montreux for Quincy Jones – www.reuters.com/article/2014/07/17/us-music-montreux-wonder-idUSKBNOFMO4A20140717

Rolling Stone, Stevie Wonder Biography – www.rollingstone.com/music/artists/stevie-wonder/biography

Rolling Stone, Songs in the Key of Life, Stevie Wonder – www.rollingstone.com/music/music/albumreviews/songs-in-the-key-of-life-19761216

Rock & Roll Hall of Fame, Stevie Wonder Biography – www.rockhall.com/inductees/stevie-wonder/bio

Star Pulse.com, Stevie Wonder Biography – www.starpulse.com/music/Wonder_Stevie/Biography

Stevie Wonder, Stevie Wonder Biography – www.stevie-wonder.net/bio.htm

Stevie Wonder, www.steviewonder.org.uk/discography/albums/stevie-at-the-beach/lyric7.htm

Super Seventies.com, Innervisions, Stevie Wonder – www.superseventies.com/spwonderstevie1.htm

The New York Times, Stevie Wonder Music Banned in South Africa – www.nytimes.com/1985/03/27/arts/stevie-wonder-music-banned-in-South-Africa.html

Printed in Great Britain
by Amazon